A FEELING OF WORTH

A Manifesto for Mending Our Broken World

A FEELING OF WORTH

A Manifesto for Mending Our Broken World

BAY JORDAN

First Published In Great Britain 2009
by www.BookShaker.com

To my wife and children.

The people whose love makes my life so worthwhile.

Contents

Introduction

"God, give me the strength to change the things that I can, the serenity to accept the things I cannot and the wisdom to know the difference."

REINHOLD NIEBUHR 1892-1971: AMERICAN THEOLOGIAN

This book has been fifteen years in gestation. The quote above is one of the reasons for that, because this book ultimately deals with issues that I appear to have little power to change. Consequently there has been a little voice inside my head saying that it was pointless and who was I to think that my ideas had any merit or that the world might be interested in them? Yet, like most people, these issues are things that affect me, and consequently there has been a mounting sense that I have an obligation to at least try to do something.

Then I came across another quote that created a different voice inside my head telling me that I should go ahead.

"I always wondered why somebody didn't do something about that. Then I realised I was somebody." Lily Tomlin

So I took the plunge and started writing. I was actually quite pleased with the way it was going and thought that I was making some good sense and would really help change the world. Unfortunately the need to earn a living took a more pressing hold and I found myself obliged to stop for a while. That was in April 2007 and needless to say the break proved to be longer than I expected. For, while I wasn't writing I found that first voice started to dominate again, this time saying, "You are just being pessimistic. Nobody is going to want to read that and it certainly isn't going to change things." So the book just sat in the drawer.

1

Introduction

Then the financial crisis struck, causing the credit crunch and the whole global economy to go into meltdown. Now the other voice in my head popped up and said, "You see! You were right about everything you said was wrong. You should never have stopped." And the first voice said, "But you did, and now the opportunity is gone. Who wants to read a prophecy about something that is going to happen after it has already happened?" To which the wannabe writer responded, "Ah yes, but now you might have an audience that is more ready to consider your solutions! You might at least be able now to 'make a difference' and contribute to making the world a better place."

So, as you can see, the upshot of all this is that the second voice has won! I don't know whether all my ideas are brilliant, or just some of them or even none of them. I just know that they deserve as much as anyone's to be expressed, and hopefully the few trees that die as a result won't have died in vain.

One of the consequences, however, of this protracted mental argument has been the difficulty of adjusting what I had already written to take account of what has subsequently happened. This has been one of my biggest challenges. I have tried to make changes wherever I could, but I am sure there are instances when my synchronisation is not all it should be. However, I am inclined to think there is no need to apologise for that, and that it might just give the whole work more credibility and convince you that I am not just climbing on the bandwagon, as one of the many now coming forward to claim that they had long predicted this. Indeed, I hope my suggestions will prove more insightful and constructive than any being made by people looking to profit out of adversity, precisely because they have been considered for so long. I do apologise, however, if I am wrong about needing to apologise.

There is one thing that I am particularly grateful to the delay for. In the last few weeks I met a new colleague, Alistair Lobo, who introduced me to his "Be, Do, Have, Purpose, Vision, Mission" diagram. This is his copyrighted material and he is shortly to publish his own book around these concepts, but he has given me permission to use it. In my opinion, even if you think every word I have written is a complete waste of time and you want to go out and hug the nearest tree in sympathy, this alone is worth the price of the book!

It might help if I explain that his diagram actually gives a greater insight into my motives for writing this book. I have light-heartedly described the mental arguments that I had about writing it, but the diagram actually depicts the process that I went through intuitively without even knowing about its existence. In that sense it is an affirmation, but I share it with you, both in the hope that it will help each and every reader individually, and because it encapsulates what I am trying to achieve with this book. It is effectively a framework around which I unconsciously built my ideas and should be kept in mind at all times when these, or any other solutions, are considered.

© Certain Progress Consultants

Let's now put this in context.

LIFE

Purpose:

Whether my time on earth is just a chapter in my existence or all there is, I believe my life has a purpose. I have been given no precise idea or road map that tells me what that purpose is, but it entails being the best I can in whatever situation I find myself. This requires identifying, developing and utilising whatever skills I have in these situations as they demand, and as a result of this I have come to identify my purpose as being to help improve things. My purpose in writing the book is to express my own being more directly. I need to apply my qualities, talents and skills to finding answers to these issues.

Vision:

My vision is to develop and shape opportunities where I can best use these talents and skills to fulfil my purpose.

Mission:

My mission is to identify the various ways in which I can fulfil that vision. Here I fold in what I learned from reading Stephen Covey's "Seven Habits of Highly Effective People" and identify all the various roles I have in life - son, father, husband, brother, businessman etc. - and try to identify a mission for each role.

BUSINESS

This is the map I followed when I set up my consultancy business.

Purpose:

My purpose is to use my skills in business situations where businesses are facing problems.

Vision:

My vision is for businesses to run smoothly and harmoniously. Where issues are identified they are effectively addressed and the organisations themselves operate as one aligned team.

Mission:

My mission is to identify the specific ways in which to do this; e.g. strategy, change-management, etc.

The outcome of this should be happier workplaces for my clients and an income that enables me to have some balance in my life to fulfil all my various roles and enjoy the things that life has to offer.

BOOK

So it is natural that I should have used this approach too when it came to writing this book.

Purpose:

I have had issues with some of the circumstances and situations I have encountered during my life journey. As a result I have identified ways that they could be improved. I would not be doing myself justice or living to my purpose if I did not voice my ideas as to how they could be improved.

Vision:

My vision is that these solutions will help reshape the way the world operates and improve the way we live.

Mission:

My mission is thus to share these ideas as widely as possible. This will identify like-minded people who feel strongly that these ideas have merit and who will add their own to modify and improve them. Then, wherever necessary or desirable, people will work together to make them happen, even if it is long after my own life has come to an end.

Thus the book seems to be the ideal way to align these elements to deliver an outcome that sees the world as a better place for all humankind.

This may seem overly ambitious, and it is certainly a very long way removed from Niebuhr's advice quoted right at the beginning, but it seems to be justified by the mess the world has got itself into and the chickens that are now coming home to roost.

However, there is further justification. You see, our feeling of worth ultimately derives from the extent to which we are able to fulfil our purpose. But, perhaps paradoxically, this can only happen when our purpose is fixed on something outside of ourselves. This is because, ultimately, value is not unilateral. A miser's money actually has no value until it is brought out of its hiding place and used. Well the same applies to our qualities and abilities; unless we use them they are worthless. But their worth comes from sharing them or using them to benefit others. It is other's appreciation of our qualities that makes them valuable and it is this appreciation that flames our feeling of self-worth. Without appreciation, or a sense of being useful, our feeling of worth flickers and dies.

Maslow's hierarchy identified a sequence of human needs, culminating in self-actualisation. This list, however, is not hierarchical at all and this fulfilment - this feeling of worth - is the most basic spiritual need and is ultimately as important as the air we breathe. You need only look at any young toddler's efforts to get parental attention and approval to understand this.

This, I believe, is what the world today has lost. Our focus has been all on our own wants and desires and we have found them insufficient to satisfy these more basic essentials. Consequently our feeling of worth has diminished to such an extent that we seem to be permanently dissatisfied. Again Lily Tomlin expresses it beautifully: *"The trouble with the rat race is that, even if you win, you are still a rat."*

As I said, I didn't know about this model of Alistair Lobo's, but nevertheless seem to have followed it intuitively, and it has certainly worked for me. However, in following it, I have also learned that the focus has to be external for what I am doing to have any real meaning or bring any true satisfaction.

I do not know to what extent I have, consciously or sub-consciously, followed this approach in the course of this book. Having now discovered it I have, however, used it at the end in an effort to bring my thoughts to a constructive conclusion that makes some kind of sense. I would ask you to try to use it yourselves as you read the book. That way you will hopefully be able to add more value to these ideas and enable me to fulfil my mission and reshape the world.

The fact is that Niebuhr was wrong. It was Einstein who said, *"The world is a dangerous place; not because of the people who are evil, but because of the people who don't' do anything about it."* We are all in this world together and as such we have joint responsibility for what happens. If we accept that there are some human activities which we cannot influence and just leave to others, we find they get hijacked and become corrupt and dangerous, and ultimately put everything we believe in at risk. At the same time, it destroys our own feeling of worth.

PART 1
Scene-Set

CHAPTER ONE

Smarter Than Frogs?

"The art of life lies in a constant readjustment to our surroundings."

OKAKURA KAKUZO

Perhaps; but what sort of life? In a world of constantly accelerating change it might be more accurate to describe the constant readjustment to our surroundings as the "art of survival" rather than the "art of life." Nor is this an original thought, for around the same time Kakuzo was philosophising, Charles Darwin was already proclaiming that, *"It is not the strongest of the species that survive, nor the most intelligent, but the one most responsive to change."*

This has become accepted wisdom, and the speed of change in modern western society is creating an ever-increasing awareness of both change itself and the need to manage it more effectively. Whereas historically it was gradual and often even barely perceptible, its current speed now makes the pace of change a primary factor of progress in its own right.

In his book "The Age of Unreason" Charles Handy gives the example of the frog that, when put in water that is slowly heated, will eventually allow itself be boiled to death. He builds on this illustration to make the point that, *"We, too, will not survive if we don't respond to the radical way in which the world is changing."* The analogy certainly serves to make a point. However, it may not be totally appropriate, for the frog's problem is not radical change, but rather gradual change and its complete unawareness of it: either of what is happening or of the danger it poses. In stark contrast we are so well aware of the changes happening around us that we could never be lulled into the same apathy or false sense of security. Or could we?

There is a delightful example in the Calvin & Hobbs cartoon strip where Calvin says to Hobbs, *"Know what's weird? Day by day nothing seems to change, but pretty soon everything's different. You just go about your business and one day realise you're not the same person you used to be. People change whether they decide to or not."* What if the biggest danger facing us is not the one of "radical" change, but rather the gradual day-to-day changes that imperceptibly but inexorably alter our circumstances and reshapes our environment? After all, in the frog's case it is only the change in water temperature that proves to be fatal. Perhaps that frog, basking in the warming water and delighted with its circumstances, is simply thinking to itself, *"This is really nice. I'll just wallow for a few minutes longer and jump out when and if it gets too warm."* Could we be facing an equivalent threat? And if so, are we any more alert and responsive than the frog?

After all, humankind's ability to adapt to revolutionary change has been proven, but at the end of the day, revolutionary change has been largely situational; the consequences of humankind changing its own environment. It's all very well basking in the glorious belief of being the most intelligent creature in the animal kingdom but, if Darwin is correct, that fact alone will not guarantee our survival. In fact our self-satisfaction with our own intelligence and belief that we can apply it to modify our circumstances could turn out to be our greatest danger, and the very cause of our ultimate failure to do so. Are we really sure that we are any smarter than that frog? The "credit crunch" would suggest not.

There is no doubt that we think we are. The problem is we really don't know, because we do not have much of a track record on evolutionary change, simply because human history really is not old enough to allow judgement as to how well we, as a species, handle it. And, because of our dominance over our environment, there is a great danger of thinking either that all change is man-induced or, if not, that we are still capable of meeting any challenges that may be presented. Thus not being alert to other possibilities is quite conceivable.

Think for a moment of the before and after pictures of a masterpiece painting that has just been cleaned and restored. It is hard to believe that they are one and the same. Yet, the fact is, over the passage of time, an accumulation of dirt and grime builds up a veneer that completely dulls the intrinsic nature, beauty and quality of any work. The process, however, is so gradual that the owner and regular viewer alike do not notice and remain oblivious to its degradation and the rich detail and qualities of colour and light which are being lost. It is only when someone comes along with a fresh pair of eyes and a memory of what it used to be, or an understanding of what the picture should look like, that an awareness of the need for restoration develops. It then takes a lot of love, care and patience to bring the work back to something that more closely resembles the original.

This provides a useful analogy for life generally, and for the framework on which society hangs specifically; particularly the social, political and legal systems.

Over the course of time laws are tweaked and systems are modified in efforts to improve social conditions. Each change, however, tends to modify what has been done before and successive efforts result in concepts moving further away from the original. They become increasingly blurred by the various philosophical niceties that well-intentioned people try to superimpose. Consequently, things evolve some distance away from the original. They become more complex and confused, and the desired results ever more difficult to achieve.

Paradoxically, the inherent danger of this is a tendency to try to simplify, with the result that attention becomes increasingly focused on symptoms. As things become more and more complex there is a natural tendency to focus either on the things that are most important to us personally or those that affect us the most – which might or might not be one and the same. Focus, by definition, entails looking at things with a narrower perspective and consequently issues come into greater relief. But as they do our thinking, by contrast, tends to become more shallow and superficial. As it does, so both the issues and their potential solutions appear to become more obvious. Compounded by the growing awareness of change and the need to "adapt or die" such thinking fosters a passion for "quick fix" solutions. Unfortunately, this exacerbates the poor quality of the analysis and leaves us blind to the fact that we may actually be addressing symptoms rather than the causes of problems.

This shortcoming is starting to be recognised, not least by Peter Senge who, in his book "The Fifth Discipline", makes the case for more systemic thinking. He warns, *"Beware the symptomatic solution. Solutions that address only the symptoms of problems and not fundamental causes tend to have short term benefits at best. In the long term the problem resurfaces and there is increased pressure for symptomatic response. Meanwhile the capacity for fundamental solutions can atrophy."*[1] If you accept this at face value you can argue that the predicament is pervasive, and is evidenced by the increasing inability to find long-term solutions to problems. Increasing calls, in all walks of life, for a shift "back to basics" perhaps exemplifies this. Often, however, we undertake remedies with a specific focus or objective in mind which, precisely because we are looking at the problem in

---

[1] Peter Senge "The Fifth "Discipline" Random House January 2007 (This is actually a revised edition and differs slightly from the earlier edition from which the quote was taken)

isolation, means we concentrate on the symptoms and consequently compound the problem rather than solve it.

Accordingly, the second part of this book explores this phenomenon and some of the consequences. It takes a deeper look at society and some of the ways in which, like a painting, it has lost its lustre. We will look at how years of accumulated symptomatic solutions – well-intended policy changes, layered one upon the other without proper priming – have (mixing metaphors terribly) had a water-heating effect and brought us to a point of crisis where we need a complete overhaul if we are to survive.

After we have seen the accumulated "dirt", its effects and what is possible if it is removed, part three suggests how things could be turned around and the danger reduced. It presents ideas for more systemic change. Hopefully these will create an environment where we are more alert to such gradual change and its risks, and leave us better equipped to meet the dangers posed by the more radical changes that (despite everything that has been said) might still be the threat portrayed by Handy and other leading thinkers of our day.

Perhaps the true "art of life" is to appreciate the interconnection and interdependence of all living things and to ensure that we do nothing to upset the equilibrium that sustains it. This may immediately bring the subject of global warming to mind, but this is an ideal and topical example of the consequences of the kind of thinking this book is challenging. Global warming is the perfect pointer, illustrating just how similar our predicament is to that frog's, and how blissfully oblivious humankind is capable of being – despite our much acclaimed superior intelligence.

However, before we leap to the conclusion that we are no smarter than frogs, there may be another reason we only act when we reach a crisis point. Perhaps we are just insane. After all, while perhaps psychologically or scientifically questionable, one popular definition of insanity is, *"repeating the same thing over and over again and expecting a different outcome."*[2]

Of course some will dispute this definition and argue that it is actually the definition of persistence, and that persistence is a virtue, à la the old adage, "If at first you don't succeed, try and try again." The key here would seem to be the expectancy. But, regardless of the objective, it is surely insane to persist in any activity when the outcome is undesirable or inadequate. In this case then, the definition does not actually depend on the expectation but rather on the unchanging nature of the action. We can thus re-define insanity quite simply as, *"the ongoing repetition of action when change is warranted."*

So there are now two possibilities – either we are stupid or we are crazy! Of course it doesn't really matter whether the issue is foolishness or insanity, does it? This merely shows how easy it is to get sidetracked and start looking at the symptoms rather than causes of the problems. The fact still remains that there are problems that are not being faced up to and dealt with. We need to get to grips with this as a matter of some urgency. So let's now start considering some of these problems.

---

[2] The source of this piece of popular wisdom is uncertain and is variously attributed to Benjamin Franklin and HW Longfellow and possibly others.

PART 2
Problems

CHAPTER TWO

The Failure of Democracy

"No one pretends that democracy is perfect or all-wise. Indeed it has been said that democracy is the worst form of government except all those other forms that have been tried from time to time."

WINSTON CHURCHILL

It is sixty years since Churchill made that statement in parliament. His words clearly indicate a widespread recognition, even then, that democracy was not a panacea. Yet, despite this, little if anything has been done to improve it. In fact, the earlier definition of insanity as persistence in doing the same thing in the face of evidence that change is needed certainly seems to apply here. The only change to the western world's perspective of democracy seems to be that we have lost sight of its imperfections altogether.

Efforts to enforce democracy in countries where alternative systems of government prevail certainly seem to preclude any acceptance of possible shortcomings. They indicate a zeal that, rather ironically, runs completely counter to the very principles of democracy. After all, going to war to impose democracy on countries where it is an alien culture is hardly in keeping with the underlying spirit of Voltaire's declaration, *"I disapprove of everything you say, but will defend to the death your right to say it!"* [3]

---

[3] Attributed to Voltaire (Francois-Marie Arouet) but apparently not found in any of his writings.

Needless to say, there are a number of fundamental issues that challenge this evangelical fervour. Even if we accept that these endeavours to spread democracy are genuine, and not the hidden commercial ambitions that are often claimed, they appear to be misplaced as well as misguided.

THE VOCAL MINORITY

One major, intrinsic weakness of democracy is the disproportionate power wielded by the people who "shout the loudest." Although they are recognised as "the vocal minority" the extent of their ability to influence others and shape outcomes is often under-estimated.

Damian Hughes, author of the book "Liquid Thinking"[4] and one of the key instigators of transformation in Unilever's Port Sunlight operation, identifies four types of behaviours when it comes to change which he uses to categorise people. He maintains that to effect change it is essential to understand and be able to manage them all.

	POSITIVE	NEGATIVE
ACTIVE	**PLAYERS** Make it happen	**TERRORISTS** Stop it
PASSIVE	**SPECTATORS** Hope it / Want it	**CORPSES** No idea / Don't care

---

[4] Deanprint Ltd 2005 ISBN 0-9551848-0-0

This nomenclature is idiomatic and so does not describe people generally but rather their response or attitude to specific issues. As a result they are universal categories that apply to any situation where people are required to make a judgement. The vertical axis divides those who are positive about things from those who are negative or indifferent, while the horizontal axis divides the active and the passive. The grid's application to specific situations makes it rather an inappropriate tool for analysing abstract or complex concepts, so it is inappropriate for looking at democracy in its entirety, but it does provide some useful insights.

The issue from a democratic perspective is that those who feel strongly – those on the top half of the matrix – often do their best to make their opinion the one that carries the day. While there is absolutely nothing wrong with conviction which leads to activism – as Hughes indicates, this is vital to change and hence (always assuming that change is positive) to progress – there is a danger of polarisation between opposing viewpoints. In fact it seems that this is increasingly the case, resulting in escalating violence of the sort typified by pro-life groups in the US and animal rights activists in the UK. Thus the increasing intolerance in society, typified by such indicators as public debates where the parties refuse to listen and talk over one another; road rage; etc. results not only in the fundamental erosion of the underlying principles of democracy, but the issues themselves assuming a disproportionate significance and possibly distorting the whole political agenda.

This may not seem too serious but think of the old proverb, *"Empty vessels make the most noise"*. In such situations there is a danger of succumbing to the lowest rather than highest aspirations of human governance.

ADVERSARIAL POLITICS

Closely related to this, perhaps more so than we would like to think, is the western democratic tradition of party politics.

Can there be anything less inspiring and more demeaning than watching elected representatives hurling abuse at each other across the chambers of parliament like overgrown schoolboys? The idea of Socratic debate gets completely sublimated in partisan point scoring and finger pointing. Each side blames the other for the ills of the country and political execution comprises a zigzag pattern akin to a tacking yacht as each incoming government does all it can to undo the actions of its predecessor. This is often done covertly as it cannot be done overtly.

Britain and the United States are perhaps the worst for partisan politics. The dominance of their respective parties, each with a long history, means there is a danger of party interests taking precedence over national interests. However, the instability of parliaments elected through proportional representation à la Italy, hardly offers an inspiring alternative.

POLITICAL FUNDING

Strongly linked to this is the matter of funding of political parties. This plays a fundamental part in the integrity of the democratic process and so poses a number of questions.

It is perhaps unfair to claim that there is a lack of general awareness of this issue and that it thus warrants a place amongst the determinants of insanity. Yet it reached new levels of prominence in the UK with the 2006 "loans for peerages" scandal, that saw Tony Blair become the first Prime Minister in British history to be interviewed by the police as part of a criminal investigation while in office. Yet one can only wonder whether he is just the first to have mishandled the process to such an extent that he aroused suspicion.

The problem is that political parties operate just like any other organisation: they need money to remain viable. Electioneering, particularly in this age of mass communication, is very costly and all parties are struggling to fund the "air-time" to get their message across and raise awareness of the issues. This makes them increasingly anxious to identify new sources of funding and increases the risk of choosing options that do not necessarily accord with true democratic values, as evidenced by this scandal. Increasing use is being made of the internet, but this undermines a very crucial element of democratic politics – the personal touch.

The 2008 US election also begs the question when the two parties spent nearly a trillion dollars ($1,000,000,000,000) on their campaigns, with one party's fund raising enabled them to outspend the other by more than two to one. While the absolute spend seems mind-boggling, one should not overlook that this amounted only to about $3 per head of population. The disparity of the spending, however, does make it look like the result was bought.

POLITICAL LOBBYING

Lobbying could be said to be the vocal minority in formalised action, but of course it is much more than this. In many ways it is effectively a combination of all of the above, and does tend to be more widely recognised as an issue – often as the result of hard-hitting television programmes and the cinema. These capture the imagination and interest and can fill a useful role. There is often a danger that they are seen either as purely fictional and the potential peril thereby diminished through an "it-could-never-happen-here" attitude or, equally risky, a dismissal of "subversive" writers and producers, carried away by a sense of self-importance.

While generally legal and conscientious efforts are made, or appear to be made to control lobbying, the practical difficulties of policing it make this very difficult. Even where there are grounds for suspicion, hard evidence of irregularities can be very hard to come by. Lobbying not only provides a vehicle for the vocal minority to ensure that their opinions are voiced, but major business corporations also use it to promote their business interests. They justify it on the grounds that it is an essential part of establishing or sustaining their market, providing jobs, safeguarding national interests etc. – you fill in the appropriate blank. The problem is that often it is the lobbyist with the biggest budget who stands to win through. This is definitely contrary to basic democracy and it is therefore ultimately quite unlikely to be in the best interests of the greater population at large.

LACK OF ACCOUNTABILITY

There is unquestionably an awareness, and possibly even a growing one, of some if not all of the above issues. Yet they do not form a complete list.

One of the most pervasive challenges threatening to undermine traditional democratic values is something perhaps best described as a "lack of accountability." This broad heading covers two distinct elements:

- The decline of standards of personal integrity; and
- The erosion of political consequence.

DECLINING PERSONAL INTEGRITY

This is an area where I may be in danger of being accused of looking at the past through rose tinted spectacles. There does, however, seem to be a greater proclivity for those in public office to disregard public opinion and "the taint of scandal" and carry on regardless, where previously they would have resigned as soon as the first accusation was made, regardless of whether the claim was well-founded or not. This may well be nothing more than a more active and far-reaching press identifying and exposing more than was ever uncovered historically, but I think there is more to it than that.

This old attitude could be attributed to a greater respect for the position and ensuring that "the office" did not come into disrepute – a civilian equivalent of saluting the rank rather than the person. In some ways this seems ludicrous. After all it is not the position or the rank that misbehaves! So, while it is quite reasonable to accord the attainment of position with the respect it deserves, it is only appropriate that the incumbent should continue to earn that respect by virtue of the manner in which they perform their role. This means they must be held accountable. The risk of having too much respect for their position creates a very real danger, figuratively, of the incumbent getting away with murder rather than risk damaging "the office".

Maybe the pendulum has swung too far the other way. Those in elected positions have a duty of trust to those who elected them. If there is any ground for suspecting them of misbehaving or failing, effectively or morally, to perform their role to the high standard expected, and of which they are presumed capable, they should immediately resign or be suspended until such time as the matter is resolved. Yet, increasingly there is a tendency in such situations for people to remain in their posts regardless – either until the pressure to go becomes irresistible, or until even more damning evidence comes to light.

An extreme example of this is President Clinton, with his famous untruth that *"I did not have sex with that woman"*. The pursuit of Clinton was possibly an extreme example of "terrorism" as depicted earlier but, regardless of how one feels about whether the affair should ever have escalated to the level it did, Clinton's behaviour was unacceptable. His statement was intrinsically no different to Nixon's initial disclaimer regarding Watergate, yet Nixon resigned whereas

Clinton did not. Whatever the reasons for his intransigence, there can be little doubt of the damage the whole affair did:

- To "the office" of president;

- To the sense of patriotic pride that Americans feel towards their country; and

- To the wider perception of the US by the world as a whole.

As the prime example and self-proclaimed "leader of western democracy", this has to have damaged democracy too.

EROSION OF POLITICAL CONSEQUENCE

That example could also be said to be indicative of an erosion of political consequence, but this issue runs considerably deeper. The basic premise of western democracy is that elected officers are accountable to their electorate. Thus their failure to properly represent the electorate's interests and aspirations should result in the loss of office. Yet it seems that increasingly this is not the case.

One needs look no further than the European parliament for evidence of this. There is only a tenuous link between voters and their representatives and certainly no way that the electorate can remove an MEP. Furthermore, it appears fashionable to regard as extremist anyone who opposes participation in Europe. Yet there are fundamental questions that do need to be answered as to the extent to which member states have sublimated their national sovereignty. With European law taking precedence over national law and MEPs not being accountable to their own national electorate, democracy definitely appears to be on the decline in Europe.

PUBLIC DISILLUSIONMENT

Now, whether or not you agree with all these factors, one issue for which there is clear empirical evidence is increasing voter apathy. Turnouts at elections continue to decline. While there are a number of reasons for this, they could arguably all be said to be rooted in these points.

In a recent article in the Sunday Times[5] Lord Saatchi, former chairman of the Conservative Party and the author of the Centre for Policy Studies pamphlet "In Praise of Ideology", quotes statistics showing that membership in political parties has declined by 2.5 million between the 1950s and today. Voter turnout has declined from 80% to 60% over the same period. Saatchi attributes this apathy to *"the barren landscape of the 'centre ground' to which all political parties have retreated"*. He argues that, *"the 'centre ground' has become the conspicuous feature of the age – the equivalent of a political law of gravity – as in the popular injunction: 'You only win elections from the centre ground.'"*

This is an erudite summary of the frequently heard statement, "What's the difference, they (politicians) are all the same!" As such it undoubtedly has validity, but in identifying this convergence as an issue and calling for more "ideology" as a solution, Saatchi is missing a vital point.

Undoubtedly lack of political differentiation creates boring politics and causes people to lose interest. Equally certainly, the underlying pragmatism suggests a great desire to attain and hold office rather than commit to principles. The perception of self-interest is compounded by regular scandals involving politicians from all parties. This breeds cynicism and distrust, and ultimately gives rise to the type of apathy currently being witnessed.

---

[5] "Come on then, we need a political punch-up" Sunday Times 7th January 2007

But, as we have seen, the issues run considerably deeper. Saatchi's call for more ideology and "a political punch-up" is an attempt to fix a symptom rather than cause of the problem. Democracy – government "of the people, for the people, by the people" – requires participation. Politics ultimately deals with the management of public affairs and the lack of participation by people in matters which directly affect them indicates a complete sense of powerlessness. Harking back to Damian Hughes' matrix, we are seeing more and more people becoming "corpses". Why?

This can only happen when people lose their sense of "worth" and become automatons. It runs much deeper than a simple lack of ideology, particularly when Saatchi himself says, *"The British People are now so knowledgeable that they approximate to what economists call, 'the perfect market', i.e. perfect knowledge and perfect ability to use it."*[6] This makes the situation even more serious for it actually points to a dangerous defect in the market which makes it very far from perfect. History abounds with examples of what happens when reasonable people become apathetic. Democracy itself is clearly under siege – for all the reasons outlined and perhaps more – and fresh ideas are needed.

---

[6] Ibid

CHAPTER THREE

The Failure of Capitalism

"Normally speaking, it may be said that the forces of a capitalist society, if left unchecked, tend to make the rich richer and the poor poorer and thus increase the gap between them."

JAWAHARLAL NEHRU

Those words of nearly fifty years ago now seem to be remarkably prophetic. There is frequent reference to the fact that wealth is increasingly confined to a smaller percentage of the world's population. Yet it hardly takes clairvoyance to recognise the inevitably of this when one considers that sex is often the only recreational activity available to the poor and hence the almost guaranteed population growth in poorer countries. The disparity in population growth alone ensures this.

The problem is, though, that wealth is at best a subjective term and therefore very much smoke and mirrors or a mirage. Consider for a moment: a Wall Street crash that saw the value of Microsoft shares plummet to next to nothing would simply wipe out a large part of Bill Gates' 'wealth'. Whether he would still be the richest man in the world would depend on the effect of the crash on his closest rivals to that claim. Would it affect him otherwise? Almost certainly yes, but only to the extent it altered his ability to meet his historical obligations and to fund future expenditure. He would still have his mansion, his plane, his yacht, his cars and all his other tangible assets. A side effect, however, would be to dramatically increase the poor's proportion of the world's wealth. Their status would thus have significantly improved without changing their circumstances one iota.

This analogy exemplifies the problem with traditional measures and statistics. We can tie ourselves in all sorts of knots as a result, over nonsensical issues that, in the greater scheme of things, are totally irrelevant. This is typified by the British obsession for league tables, with tables being used to measure the relative performance of schools, universities, hospitals and possibly even police forces.

There is a tremendous irony in a school system where it is considered inappropriate to "stream" children according to their relative abilities as this might send out the wrong message and undermine their confidence, but okay to disparage a whole school because it fared poorly in the league tables. Schools bask in the achievement of moving a few places up the table while there is pandemonium and panic when they move down the tables, and it seems that little consideration is given to the fact that student intake calibres can and do vary from year to year. Nor does there seem to be any consideration of how narrow the margins are and how little it takes to move up or down in the tables. One student having a bad exam result, perhaps because of a situation at home or because they slept badly or felt unwell on the day, can have a completely disproportionate effect and result in the school being a number of places lower on the table than it might otherwise have been.

The situation for hospitals must be even worse, where the results are likely to be skewed by the mix of patient ailments and the severity thereof. The tragedy is that these measures become paramount, affecting lives, careers and people's self-esteem simply because no other measure exists.

Wealth has always been difficult to measure not only because it is relative and very often perceived to be earned at someone else's expense, but also because it is subjective. The following delightful story illustrates this perfectly.

An American investment banker was at the pier of a small coastal Mexican village when a small boat with just one fisherman docked. Inside the small boat were several large yellow fin tuna. The American complimented the Mexican on the quality of his fish and asked how long it took to catch them.

The Mexican replied, "Only a little while."

The American then asked why didn't he stay out longer and catch more fish?

The Mexican said he had enough to support his family's immediate needs.

The American then asked, "But what do you do with the rest of your time?"

The Mexican fisherman said, "I sleep late, fish a little, play with my children, take siesta with my wife, Maria, stroll into the village each evening where I sip wine and play guitar with my amigos, I have a full and busy life."

The American scoffed, "I am a Harvard MBA and could help you. You should spend more time fishing and with the proceeds, buy a bigger boat. With the proceeds from the bigger boat you could buy several boats, eventually you would have a fleet of fishing boats. Instead of selling your catch to a middleman you would sell directly to the processor, eventually opening your own cannery. You would control the product, processing and distribution. You would need to leave this small coastal fishing village and move to Mexico City, then LA and eventually NYC where you will run your expanding enterprise."

The Mexican fisherman asked, "But, how long will this all take?"

To which the American replied, "15-20 years."

"But what then?"

The American laughed and said that's the best part. "When the time is right you would announce an IPO and sell your company stock to the public and become very rich, you would make millions."

"Millions... Then what?"

The American said, "Then you would retire. Move to a small coastal fishing village where you would sleep late, fish a little, play with your kids, take siesta with your wife, stroll to the village in the evenings where you could sip wine and play your guitar with your amigos."

This is in no way intended to deny that there is poverty and injustice in the world, but simply to convey that there is a danger of confusing wealth with quality of life, or of falling into the trap that the investment banker did of thinking that quality of life is *dependent* on wealth.

The fact is that at the start of the 21st Century we in the western world have resources that our predecessors could not have dreamed of. We have higher incomes, more leisure, greater entertainment, unparalleled opportunities to travel and do exotic things and a greater life expectancy than at any time since the flood. Yet we are perhaps more dissatisfied than any generation in human history. We have overcome the diseases that ravaged our forebears and yet there is probably more illness than ever before, and we succumb to new or more virulent ones. "Stress" was virtually unknown in our parents' generation, and yet is has become a pervasive epidemic in the early 21st Century, and is being blamed for a range of society's ills. As depicted earlier, incidents of air rage, road rage, and other symptoms of intolerance and lack of respect for our fellow human beings are increasingly prevalent and are all attributed to our being "stressed". So what is going wrong?

THE CAPITALIST PHILOSOPHY

To begin to understand this it is useful to go right back to basics and understand the nature of capitalism.

The capitalist philosophy is, in essence, premised on three fundamental principles – namely that:

1. A reasonable person will pay a price equivalent to their perceived value for any goods or service, recognising that this price includes the cost to the seller plus an element of profit necessary to enable them to fund their own needs;

2. Market forces, if not interfered with, will ensure the most economically efficient use of resources; and

3. The most economically efficient use of resources is self-evidently best for the economy as a whole and hence ultimately best for the individual.

These do, on the surface anyway, make eminent sense. Starting from the concept that needs have to be met from resources that are physically finite and therefore need to be optimised, it is totally logical that resources should be used efficiently while the cost of resources and the profit incentives *ought* to ensure that they are not wasted. And, while anti-capitalists criticise the profit ethic, it does provide a perfectly sensible mechanism for addressing the individual need – at least for all but the incapable.

Evidence would also suggest that they work. Capitalism came to the fore with the Industrial Revolution and has been a significant force in raising general standards of living, particularly in the western hemisphere where it had it roots. This is perhaps borne out by the economist Joan Robinson, who in 1960 claimed, *"Current experience suggests socialism is not a stage beyond capitalism but a substitute for it – a means by which the nations which did not share in the Industrial Revolution can imitate its technical achievements; a means to achieve rapid accumulation under a different set of rules of the game."*

So if the principles work, something in the execution must be distorting the results, and there are indeed a number of flaws.

THE PURSUIT OF GROWTH

In its purist form economics deals with the supplying of needs. This fundamentally assumes that people will produce whatever is required to enable them to survive and no more. This, however, is not the case, and the biggest shortcoming of the capitalist system is to produce ahead of requirement. Pro-capitalists will justify this on the basis that it stems from the pursuit of efficiency, while anti-capitalists will argue that is the inevitable result of greed stimulated by the profit motive. It doesn't really matter who is right, for there is probably no case for arguing against the fact of over-production, or that this, more than anything, is responsible for the 20th Century boom and bust cycle.

The motor industry[7] is perhaps the prime example of this, and there are those who claim that there is a stockpile of unsold new cars accumulating in the remote, desert regions of the US representing a massive economic time-bomb just waiting to explode. But the motor industry are by no means the only ones, and a "you-make-them-and-we'll-sell-them" manufacturing mindset with production for inventory remains a largely unquestioned fact of life in western economies, despite organisations like Dell proving that there is an alternative.

The root of the problem is of course volume. A business needs to generate sufficient volume just to cover its overheads and move to a point where the marginal sales start to generate a profit. Consequently there are two fundamental forces which drive the business economy:

---

[7] This was written well before the collapse of the financial markets and the credit squeeze that has seen the world economy plunge into recession. I will comment on this and the general malaise of the motor industry in more detail later.

1. Increasing sales to ensure sufficient profits; and

2. Reducing unit costs to lower the break-even point to achieve profits sooner.

This applies to service and retail businesses just as it does to manufacturing, resulting in the equivalent "stack-them-high-sell-them-cheap" philosophy of many retailers and discount stores and its counterpart of increased customer traffic for supermarkets and service businesses. With no recognition of economic value or contribution, the net result of this is a spiral of chasing growth for its own sake!

These are the factors which lie behind globalisation and the increasing pace of competition in the 21st century, reinforced by technological progress, which is itself the result of efforts to optimise productivity and so reduce unit costs. What people have failed to recognise, however, is that through efforts to increase sales we have effectively removed one of the basic assumptions underpinning capitalism.

ADVERTISING – A BLESSING OR CURSE?

You will recall from earlier that one of the key principles of capitalism was that, "Market forces, if not interfered with, will ensure the most economically efficient use of resources". Yet, it could be argued that, through the creation of the advertising industry, we have created something that specifically does interfere with the market. Of course that was never the intention, but it may well be the unforeseen consequence.

The ideal of advertising is to help bring a prospective customer and a seller together for them to strike a deal. Unfortunately, the desire for growth has subverted this to the point where the intention – often freely admitted – is to stimulate desire and hence demand, the consequences of which have been questionable to say the least.

While the industry can claim to be a major player in the economy its overall effects are definitely dubious. Consider that historically a significant proportion of advertising expenditure has been spent on:

- Cigarettes and tobacco
- Alcohol
- Confectionary, cold drinks and snack food
- Medicine
- Cosmetics, beauty and related personal care products

Yet all are at least questionable.

The first three of these have all come under increasing attack for their negative effects on health and the resulting social and financial strain they place on the economy. Legislation restricting the advertising of tobacco products has been passed in many countries in Europe as a result, and with increasing concern about the problem of binge drinking and anti-social behaviour there is a chance that similar restrictions may be considered for advertising alcoholic drinks in the not too distant future, while there are already calls for seismic shifts in the "junk food" market which could affect the way it is advertised. Who knows, with global warming the same might happen to motorcar and overseas holiday advertising!

Certainly similar questions are starting to be asked about medical advertising. The connection between the mental and physical and the power of auto-suggestion has been proven for well over a hundred years and it has to be wondered whether exposure to repeated advertisements about various ailments does not contribute to their ongoing occurrence. It may sound strange to suggest that advertising could create a perverse "demand" for ill-health, but if it can be used to create a positive demand there is no reason to preclude the possibility. After all if a yawn can be contagious who knows what else is and the possibility should at least be considered and further questions asked.

In any event, as everyone knows pharmaceuticals and drugs are big business, but the dividing line between "good" drugs and bad ones is at best subjective. Drug abuse is a major cause of crime and the cost to society, both in terms of its consequences and efforts to police it, are becoming prohibitive. Yet we are compounding the problem by creating a society where much of what we do is determined by chemical substances, as typified by:

- Feeding kids drugs from the day they are born, often at the slightest ailment or – even worse – to control their behaviour.

- Setting a bad example by taking pills ourselves for "immediate" pain relief or to boost flagging energy; basically whenever we sense that all is not as we would like it.

- Freely promoting pills in the media as a panacea for just about everything.

And, if all this is not bad enough, there are debates about whether some hallucinogenic drugs should be declassified, thereby creating different classes of "illegality" and undermining the message that they are all harmful. How then can we expect our children to differentiate? How can we expect them to know what is right and what isn't?

To some extent this is all compounded by the beauty industry and the images it conveys. While there is nothing intrinsically wrong with its product, the barrage of beauty products promoted by models who, by very virtue their bodies looking good in photographs and on film, do not conform with the majority, creates false expectations and levels of self-loathing and despair that are increasingly cause for concern. This lack of worth is spawning a whole new industry of pharmaceutical remedies and cosmetic surgery that exacerbates the problem. For this reason "medical" advertising is likely to become more topical as resources get diverted into cosmetic rather than therapeutic use, particularly in an aging baby-boomer demographic where there will be a greater demand for the latter.

It could validly be argued that the beauty industry provides a natural counter to the stimulants for junk food, but nobody is asking the question whether the poor diets, lack of exercise etc. are not just a backlash by people who have despaired and given up – who, to refer back to our earlier terminology, have become "corpses" in this regard. In which case, beauty industry advertising compounds the problems rather than offsets them.

We will take a further look at some of these issues later, but the key point here is that there are issues that need to be re-assessed: blind pursuit of historic practice, including unfettered advertising, is not necessarily a good thing.

BUSINESS PROCESS IMPROVEMENT, OUTSOURCING, GLOBALISATION

As already indicated, increasing sales is not the only way business has tried to improve its performance. New technology has underpinned innovative business processes, whilst also providing access to new, previously untapped markets. This has created a cycle of new ways of doing business, new sources of co-operation and competition, new mergers and acquisitions and an outlook that regards the world as a single market. One of the most significant consequences of this has been "outsourcing" – the exporting of non-core (and sometimes even core) work to external, often foreign, companies. This has benefited businesses by reducing costs whilst simultaneously fostering the growth of future markets, following the example pioneered by Henry Ford, who paid his workers well in order to create a market (and thus more than any other single individual could be said to have kick-started global warming!)

Although arguably creating a net benefit for the economy as a whole, whilst at the same time stimulating economic development in hitherto under-developed countries, companies opting to do this have some difficulty convincing their employees of this fact. The fact is that, for most of the workers displaced by these moves, it is not easy to find replacement work or maintain their accustomed standard of living. While a few fortunate might be able to be retrained in new fields and move on, for many others the change is a severe blow. They see it as a kick in the teeth and poor reward for loyal service. So here too there is a loss of confidence and a declining sense of self-worth.

Ironically, for those employees who keep their jobs the situation hardly seems any better: even when they do not resent their misfortune in not being one of the "lucky ones" getting an attractive severance package, they lose any sense of job security but feel an expectation to work harder and produce more. This induces a sense of being exploited and not being appreciated according to their worth, which makes them increasingly disengaged and unwilling to do anything that is not in their job description. It also induces a "work-to-rule" mentality when rules govern everything and people become reluctant to use their discretion, with disastrous consequences for customer service. Ultimately, this too has to have an effect on the economy as a whole.

EASY CREDIT

Growth in sales has to a very large extent been boosted by credit sales and easy access to borrowed finance. Unlike the older generation who would never buy anything until they had saved for it and to whom debt was a shame and a slippery road to disaster or disgrace, the present generation is characterised by instant gratification. If we want something we simply go out and buy it and if we don't have the money we put in on the credit card and worry about paying for it later. Worse still, it doesn't even have to be a need.

With appetites and desires stimulated by advertising and compounded by the all-too-human need to keep up with the Jones's, the western world has continued to live beyond its means year after year. "Retail therapy" may provide temporary relief from the stress of this induced competitiveness, but it is ultimately only therapeutic for the businesses that are desperate to grow, and even then only to the extent that they can keep on growing. If, as we have just seen, this growth is only being achieved by outsourcing and developing foreign markets, it inevitably has to have a negative impact on the local economy. This, after all, is just the corollary to Henry Ford's growth philosophy. Stimulating a foreign market whilst simultaneously reducing the existing labour force in the primary economy, must unavoidably cause some shrinkage in the local economy. The argument that investment returns will compensate for this *may* be valid, but only so long as the business ownership remains in local hands, and as the foreign economy grows, so does the risk of a change and relocation of ownership, creating a risk of "reverse colonisation". Clearly debt in such circumstances is dangerous.

The problem with debt is that it has to be repaid. Yes, repayments can be spread, but the longer it takes to repay, the more it ultimately erodes wealth, particularly when the bulk of debt is for non-investment purposes. Everyone knows that by the time a mortgage is paid off the purchaser will generally have paid something like 2.5 times the purchase price of the property. This is deemed acceptable because:

- It is the only way that most people can afford to acquire their own homes; and

- At the end of the exercise one has a home, which in all likelihood has increased in value, and is something which can be passed on to the next generation.

The recent trend, however, has been for debt to be incurred for consumables. This is considerably more difficult to justify because, as the term implies, the product has a limited life-span and so the value has usually been consumed by the time the purchaser has completed paying for it, which means that a replacement item now needs to be bought. This perpetuates a cycle of debt.

That is the very worst thing about debt, because it inevitably creates a spiral that tends to be self-perpetuating. As those who are or ever have ever been in debt will know only too well, it always takes longer to get out of debt than initially anticipated. Repayment necessitates setting aside a portion of present income which means foregoing spending on something else. It thus becomes a matter of choice and individual priorities, but more often than not for those for whom the repayment amount is a significant portion of their disposable income this can be a problem because other unforeseen situations arise which create further strains on their resources. This is reasonable risk when the debt is incurred for acquiring an asset that will provide a benefit for longer than the loan period or something that will help recover its costs and/or provide a potential income stream, immediately or at some time in the future. However, when it is incurred for anything else that is not completely unavoidable it is unreasonable to the point of being totally insane.

Even worse though, is the fact that high street banks who lend the money are risk averse and so reluctant to lend to the poorer sector of society because of their high-level of non-payment. This high risk factor results in others stepping into the market and offsetting this risk by charging higher interest rates, which of course means that those least able to afford it but who, by dint of circumstance often have no choice but to borrow, end up paying considerably more for the privilege than their better off fellow citizens. Consequently, with such punitive interest rates, it is hardly any wonder that the gap between rich and poor has widened, for the debt burden for the poor creates a vicious cycle that increases rather than alleviates poverty.

Simplistically wealth may be defined as what we have less what we owe, while debt is a liability incurred against future earnings. Thus at any given time being in debt actually detracts from our individual wealth. Consequently, when debt is incurred for anything other than asset build up it actually makes us poorer. Of course when the bulk of debt is for consumer goods it not only makes us immediately poorer, but it also undermines our ability to build up assets for our future and so perpetuates an impoverished status.

Needless to say, in the kind of economy described earlier, where there is a very real danger of shrinkage, debt is an unexploded time bomb. Factor in the aging population in the western world and some of the other issues raised in this book and the problem starts to assume gargantuan proportions. Clearly capitalism in its current form is not all it is cracked up to be, and new approaches need to be found.

FORESIGHT

I have to confess to a morbid fascination in re-reading what I have written above now, in December 2008, for it was actually written in April 2007. Of course I should have rewritten it but I just couldn't bring myself to do so. Recent events completely validate everything I wrote then and there really isn't much more to add that would not be simply stating the obvious. There is probably very little to be gained by attempting to do that. The credit crunch and the economic downturn we are currently experiencing are precisely the consequences of the drive for growth that I was forecasting.

Part of the problem was that the banks and other blue-chip financial institutions figured that they could also get a share of the high-risk market by lending at more favourable rates and eliminating most of the risk by parcelling up loans and selling them on. In fact, as we now know, this just multiplied the risk and caused problems for more banks when borrowers were unable to repay. Consequently, the money has disappeared down a massive virtual sink-hole and, because of the ethereal nature of wealth described earlier, we as a society are considerably poorer. Not only have we lost some of our sense of self-worth as a result of being party to this, directly or indirectly, but we have collectively lost some of our real 'worth' to the extent this is valued in monetary terms.

These consequences are the result of human frogs bathing in water with a steadily rising temperature and being unable to jump out in time. I shall deal more with some of the consequences later, but the real tragedy of the situation is twofold:

1. That the innocent have to suffer with the guilty, for it is undoubtedly a situation that could have been avoided, where the innocent are as deeply affected as the perpetrators who should have known better.

2. That there are no consequences for those people whose actions gave rise to this chain of events, thus reinforcing my point about the lack of accountability.

Suffice to say that the situation reinforces the point that new approaches need to be found and I hope that my readers will bear with me, and consider and build on the ideas I put forward to develop effective solutions that will go some way to ensuring that capitalism is never again allowed to fail on such a scale.

The Failure of Capitalism

CHAPTER FOUR

The Failure of Socialism

"Many people feel empty, a world that seemed so strong just collapsed. Forty years have been wasted on stupid strife for the sake of an unsuccessful experiment. The values gathered together have vanished, the strategies for survival have become ridiculous. And so forty years of our lives have become a story, a bad anecdote. But it may be possible to remember these adventures with a kind of irony."

GEORGE KONRAD, LONDON, APRIL 15, 1990

"Irony" may not be quite the right word given the scale of wastage and the cost in lives and general human suffering, but it is difficult to think of any other more appropriate. There is unquestionably a certain irony in the collapse of communism, and with it the loss of credibility of the socialist ethic that underpinned it.

In the boxing ring if one fighter goes down for the count the other is automatically the winner, and because of the head-to-head nature of the ideological conflict, the fall of the Berlin Wall left capitalism as the "winner" and everyone hailing it as the new champion. The euphoria of the occasion blinded us to the fact that, as we have just seen, capitalism was not the worthy champion it appeared.

It is thus not surprising that the transition to capitalism in formerly communist countries is proving turbulent and, as the quality of the emperor's clothes is increasingly being questioned, there is a very real possibility of trying to turn back the clock. Also, despite the evident shortcomings that precipitated its failure, there are elements of socialism that remain integral to capitalist society and, while a "third way" that balances the best of capitalism and socialism may, theoretically at least, offer a desirable option, there is a risk of "cultural creep" that will give socialism a renewed energy and mean the lessons from its failure have not been learned.

THE SEEDS OF FAILURE

There may be numerous ideological differences between capitalism and socialism, but remember Joan Robinson's words quoted earlier; *"Current experience suggests socialism is not a stage beyond capitalism but a substitute for it – a means by which the nations which did not share in the Industrial Revolution can imitate its technical achievements; a means to achieve rapid accumulation under a different set of rules of the game."* They are tantamount to an admission that the primary difference was simply the use of human resources to compensate for the lack of financial or capital resources. This is borne out by the fact that communism became a force in the more populous countries like Russia and China, that did not have any democratic legacy or history of championing human rights.

More significantly, perhaps, this also challenges the perception that the conflict between capitalism and socialism was truly one of ideology. It suggests that it was rather simply one of economic competition. Certainly ideological claims that socialism is more humane and better addresses the imbalances and inequities of capitalism, do not stand up too well to scrutiny. Whatever success communism did enjoy was brought about by the exploitation of people. Why else was religious and political freedom restricted and policy enforced through strict policing and heavy-handed authority? Hardly the caring ideology its proponents aver.

The claim that socialism destroys individual initiative may just have been the anti-communist line we were fed in school, but it certainly appears to have been validated by the general atmosphere of fear and suspicion. The dour, unsmiling demeanour that was widely agreed to differentiate communist subjects from their "free-world" counterparts in the west and portrayed so bleakly in contemporary film, was as much a cliché as the old westerns. Even allowing for dramatic licence and "western propaganda" there has to be some basis for this portrayal; and the eventual collapse of the Berlin Wall certainly gives it greater credibility. And, lest anyone claim that this was simply the difference between the more hard-line communist regimes and the "true" socialists, one only needs to look at the "Winter of Discontent" and the forces that gave rise to Thatcherism in the UK to know that this is not the case and that socialism is personally and nationally debilitating.

There is clear evidence that the greater the effort to make people more equal, the more people lose their individual sense of self-worth and become demoralised and demotivated. Even today, this is recognised by all but the most dyed-in-the-wool socialists who continue to voice their concerns about the shift away from traditional party policies by "New Labour" and fail to recognise that their party would have no chance of remaining in government if any such reversion took place.

THE DRIVE TO MEDIOCRITY

One seemingly obvious reason for this is natural human competitiveness. From birth we are naturally ego-centric and, from bawling for basic needs, we soon move on to demanding our parents' attention for nearly everything we do and achieve. The early plea to "Look, Mummy!" is indicative of a desire for approval that never leaves us. As we enlarge our social circle it results in a natural competitiveness and desire to outperform others in whatever situation we find ourselves. While the degree of competitiveness may vary, the only natural forces that can erode this tendency are continually inferior performance or a realisation of a complete lack of ability or interest.

Unfortunately, there are other outside forces that can also work to undermine this innate sense, and these include both:

- A lack of appreciation; and

- A sense of futility.

It may be the classic psychological cliché to point to the delinquent child as an example of someone perpetually striving for attention and prepared to go to virtually any lengths to get it, but it nevertheless underscores the point. Similarly, it is also a proven fact that performance can, and does, deteriorate when the initial challenge wears thin.

By no stretch of the imagination are these forces unique to socialism, but they do tend to be ingrained into socialist systems. This is simply because, in seeking social justice, one of the major political arguments for socialism is greater equality. Unfortunately the quest for equality inevitably tends to stamp out individualism and so eliminates the point of striving to be different and better. Exceptional effort is unappreciated and the reward disproportionate to the amount of effort put in, which makes it seem futile. So, with little incentive to do better, the more capable tend to settle for doing the bare minimum necessary, which generally tends towards the level achieved by the less able.

Consequently the system tends to function at the level of the lowest common denominator with little to differentiate the more able from the less able. It thus creates low productivity with self-perpetuating mediocrity and, unless specific remedial action is taken, a tendency to spiral downwards rather than improve. This may well be why communism was unable to compete with capitalism over time, and eventually collapsed. The innate competitive forces of human nature created an insatiable envy in Eastern Europe that demanded change.

IS THE "WAR" REALLY OVER?

Unfortunately envy is not enough to change a decades old social, economic and political system. There is a danger that dissatisfaction with the new regime, short memories, and residual unreformed hardliners will cause a resurgence of such discredited thinking. In fact the signs are that this is already happening in Russia. Ironically, this might partly be because, without the infrastructure and the legal systems that historically protected traditional capitalism from itself and its worst elements, these systems have been wider open to exploitation. So the weaknesses that have recently been exposed in western capitalism are in fact magnified in the new eastern bloc version. So for the man in the street, it has been rather a case of exchanging one privileged class for another with no improvement, and possibly even a deterioration, in their personal circumstances.

It seems unfortunate that nationalistic competition and the lack of visionary statesmen in world politics obscured the issues and meant little was done to help and thus reduce this risk.

So the ideological conflict between capitalism and socialism is perhaps one of the best examples of shallow, symptomatic thinking and humankind's tendency to over-simplify things. This is implicit in Joan Robinson's theory that socialism or communism is just a means for disadvantaged economies to make up for their lack of capital. This theory seems to gain credibility in light of China's massive economic growth and the shift to a more capitalistic approach that is accompanying it – although it is difficult to say which came first.

Irrespective of which way round it is, China seems to show that it is possible to combine capitalist and communist thinking and that the divide is not as significant as the world has been brainwashed into believing. There may be other examples of this closer to home, for even the more overtly capitalist economies have adopted socialist policies to such an extent that they have become ingrained in policy right across the political spectrum and are no longer even challenged.

The Cold War itself might have been particularly inane but, in light of all this, any threat of a return to, or recurrence of, hostilities would be even more ludicrous.

POLITICAL CREEP

An unwritten rule of democracy is that no incoming government can undo what its predecessor has done. This makes perfect sense on two grounds:

1. The governing party is accountable to its electorate for its actions while in government. So its actions are therefore deemed to have been approved by the majority and it would therefore be wrong to simply undo them, (although of course, by dint of the new mandate received from the electorate after it has published its policy during its election campaign, the incoming government is entitled to amend what its predecessor did.)

2. To have successive governments each reversing what its predecessor did while in power would be economic lunacy.

As a result the mechanics of policy become confused and inefficient as successive governments modify them to meet their own policy objectives. Consequently there is no such thing as pure capitalism or pure socialism. The policies of each become embedded in the system as the political pendulum swings back and forth. So some socialist doctrine has become embedded in the capitalist political structure.

Two major areas spring immediately to mind, when looking for examples of how socialist thinking has "infiltrated" the capitalist model.

CENTRALISATION OF POWER

Staunch Conservatives and liberals alike continue to bemoan the growth of the "Nanny State" and the steadily growing interference of government in private life. Yet, the rush to hold the central ground and so win the popular vote to secure power means that this issue of principle gets totally sacrificed and nothing is done to stop it. Thus individual freedoms, the bedrock of democratic society, get further eroded. It is said that during Tony Blair's 10 years in office some 3,700 new statutes were put on the books, with the more highly visible examples including the bans on fox-hunting and of smoking in public places. It is hardly surprising the prison population is at an all-time high and new prisons need to be built!

The problem with this, however, is the insidious cost creep which means that more and more is spent on government. And, because their priorities are more socio-political than economic, governments are notoriously inefficient in the way they disburse money. The net result is greater overall economic inefficiency and ultimately a decline in national productivity and ergo inevitably in living standards. To date this has been largely overlooked because the consequences have not been too severe, but as the chickens come home to roost and society has to start paying for these oversights – just as it has to start paying for global warming – the competition for funds is going to increase exponentially, with all the related conflict and pressures that will create. The effect is just the same as for excessive borrowing, as described earlier, for misspent resources and waste now have to be repaid by future earnings.

SOCIAL BENEFITS

The welfare state is perhaps the perfect example of how socialistic policies have become embedded in modern capitalist society. While nobody with a modicum of humanity has any gripe with the concept of trying to help the poor or disadvantaged improve their lot in life, this has actually become an economic millstone around the country's neck, simply because, like the borrowing referred to earlier, more and more of the national income gets siphoned towards paying for this.

The real issue here is not the concept but the execution, for it has become an entitlement without any corresponding obligation. It is the reverse of the old adage: *"Give a man a fish and you give him a meal; teach a man to fish and you feed him for life"*. The former is in fact charity and no matter how well intentioned charity is, without some of the self-help element of the latter, will always ultimately destroy any vestige of self-respect the recipient may have. Consequently the existing social welfare system erodes self-respect and perpetuates a cycle of dependency. Even worse, this passes from one generation to the next, which is one reason why, in Britain at least, there is an element of society that is completely unemployable: unable to do skilled work and unwilling to do unskilled work.

This is the danger that Benjamin Franklin was alluding to when he said, *"Idleness and pride tax with a heavier hand kings and governments"*. Harsh though this may seem, the fact remains that it does represent a future time-bomb that needs to be recognised and addressed now.

In both cases the fundamental issue is one of waste. There are limited physical resources. These demand wiser, more thoughtful usage, especially as the likelihood is that their costs will rise. But the aging population and shrinking workforce of western society will make it increasingly difficult to meet the increased costs. Historically economic growth has been sustained by technological development and population growth, but the changing demographics make this impossible in the near future.

The point here is not to denigrate socialism or prolong the ideological struggle of the mid-twentieth century, which in any case we have seen to be pointless and futile. The boundaries ill-defined and blurred, and the two ideologies are increasingly absorbing aspects of the other to an extent that makes the distinction irrelevant. Plus, as we are now seeing, capitalism is far from perfect and is just as culpable for the predicament in which the world finds itself. No, the real issue is simply to highlight that the water is definitely heating up significantly and we need to wake up to that fact and do something, otherwise we will end up just like that frog.

The Failure of Socialism

CHAPTER FIVE

False Profits

*"Every action has an equal
and opposite reaction."*

ISAAC NEWTON'S 3RD LAW OF MOTION

To confine this statement to a place in physics as "the third law of motion" is to do it a great disservice for it has a far wider application than just that. In fact it could be said to be one of the primary laws of nature. As we all know from our lessons in science, there is no loss from any chemical change; substances change form, but nothing is ever lost. Remember those first experiments when you placed a piece of potassium or sodium in a beaker of water and it fizzed around like an excited firework? And then subsequently proving (if memory serves correctly) that the result had been the release of oxygen?

Newton's law is thus just a limited application of that wider chemistry lesson. Every action may have a consequence; it may even change the physical and/or chemical structure of the elements involved, but at the end of the day, there is no net change in the total of the elements comprising the known universe. In arithmetical terms the total of the population of known substances remains unchanged.

NEWTON AS AN ACCOUNTANT

Looking at this from an accounting perspective may help to understand it better. Accounting is premised on the fundamental principle of double entry book-keeping, which is derived from the simple concept that any monetary transaction has two aspects. For example buying something for resale results in an increase (debit) to inventory but a reduction (credit) in cash. Thus whenever a transaction is made the accounting entry must comprise equal debits and credits and thus "balance." Hence proper accounting necessitates the books being balanced at all times. In the analogy above a reduction in potassium would be offset by an increase in oxygen and the elemental table (the environmental accounting system) would thus remain in balance.

The accounting system, however, had been in practice for some time, as it was formalised by a Franciscan monk, Fra Luca Pacioli, towards the end of the 15th Century. Newton only formulated his laws almost exactly 200 hundred years later. Thus, it would seem that the accountancy profession can quite reasonably assert that they were the first to recognise that for "every action there is an equal and opposite reaction" and so claim the bragging rights! Of course context is everything, but its application to commercial transactions as well as to the natural sciences certainly suggests that it is something that has hitherto not been fully understood or the implications recognised.

HIDDEN COSTS OR HIDDEN CONSEQUENCES?

As kids, watching potassium being put in water was a spectacle, and we could all have happily repeated the exercise over and over just to watch, but the lesson was in the consequences. It is much the same today: we carry on our adult lives more interested in the "spectacle" than the outcomes. Thus we happily use our cars or blithely discard our rubbish with little thought of the consequences. Yet, as we are learning, consequences do exist.

Think back a moment to the definition of capitalism. You will recall that one of the fundamental principles was that "a reasonable person will pay a price equivalent to their perceived value for any goods or service, recognising that the price includes the cost to the seller plus an element of profit necessary to enable them to fund their own needs". Of course that makes the asking price very subjective, because the requirement to fund the seller's need is in turn dependent on the seller's perception of their need.

Even worse, this then is susceptible to being distorted if the seller is unable to distinguish between needs and wants. This, as we have already seen, is a distinct possibility, thanks to the pressures of advertising and the competitive instinct to always keep up with or get ahead of our neighbour. Human nature is such that people will nearly always try to ask as much as they can get away with for anything they are selling. The blurring of the lines between wants and needs compounds that tendency and exacerbates the pressure on the seller to maximise what they ask for the product or service. So thank goodness we can rely on the buyer's equivalent self-interest to counter that inclination, and help ensure that price is ultimately "fair". This should help keep profits to a reasonable level and ensure that neither party is exploited.

All well and good, and here too we can see Newton's law in operation – the force of the seller to maximise their profit is matched by an equal and opposite force of the buyer to maximise theirs. However, there is a wrinkle in the works: the determination of cost.

Everyone understands that Selling Price minus Cost equals Profit: in that timeless equation that was drilled into us at school or university:

$$P = S - C$$

So we all understand that the bigger S is the bigger P will be, or the smaller C is the bigger P will be! Consequently there is another way to increase profits; and that, of course, is to decrease costs.

However, understanding this makes a significant difference, because it adds a new dimension to the tug-o'war between buyer and seller. Both seller and prospective buyer are influenced, consciously or otherwise, by their perception of cost. This helps determine the value they place on the object to begin with. But what happens when the cost is understated?

The answer is obvious: the purchaser gets a bargain! On the other hand, though, the seller feels hard done by or goes bankrupt/out of business because it turns out that they didn't make a profit at all and do not have enough to cover their own needs – or, probably, both! As you can appreciate, this risk makes it very important that the seller calculates their costs correctly.

The only time these consequences can appear be to avoided is when the true cost is not known. In such circumstances, seller and buyer alike continue in blissful ignorance and all seems well with the world. Unfortunately such ignorance cannot continue and the truth inevitably must out. Rather like a murderer who thinks he has got away with it, and is suddenly apprehended as a result of new DNA evidence, the chickens ultimately come home to roost – big time. Unfortunately, despite the passage of time, someone has to pay, but the burning question is the identity of who that will be.

What has this got to do with anything, you may be asking? Well, this of course is precisely what has happened with global warming. For decades, even centuries, humankind has failed to properly account for the resources consumed, and now we are learning the true costs, together with the fact that we are the ones who will be paying for them. Aah! So, suddenly, the burning question is no longer who, but *how*?

Perhaps you'll get an answer to that question later. (You'll have to keep reading!) Right now, it is more interesting to probe a little deeper into how this came about, and understand why we have been so froglike – as well as to take a closer look at some of the other implications. This of course means going back to Newton.

ECONOMIC IMPLICATIONS OF NEWTON'S LAW

We all understand how taking two atoms of hydrogen and one of oxygen results in the creation of one molecule of water, and thus that if one envisages a table recording all known substances, this table will be in perpetual balance. This seems to correlate well with Newton's Law, which is generally applied only to physics. Together the two point to a natural balance and a world of continuing equilibrium. In both cases the counter-action occurs in the same time frame. Thus, regardless of the complexities of what happens during the process, the equation is a simple bi-lateral one:

Action = Result or A = R

This is a natural, scientific truth, applicable throughout the universe to any physical activity. However, it leaves no room for any concept of profit. Of course, this is hardly surprising as profit is entirely a human concept, developed for commercial purposes and integrated into economic theory. There was no problem when the world was simpler and commercial activity was entirely by barter. Thus the standard transaction could thus be simplistically depicted as:

C = S

Where, from our earlier profit equation, C = the value to the buyer and S = the value to the seller. This also fits in with the earlier link identified between Newton's Law and accounting. However, the introduction of monetary exchange and the concomitant development of the concept of profit brought major complexities which have distorted the picture and which, as we are now seeing, have not been fully understood.

ECONOMICS, ACCOUNTING AND PROFITS

It could be said that humankind has an obsession for measuring. The phenomenon of creating performance tables discussed earlier is perhaps nothing more than the latest manifestation of that obsession. Measurement brings order to chaos, but in order to do so must address two basic requirements:

1. A unit of measure; and

2. Standards for comparison.

The second is particularly difficult when comparing items that are intrinsically different – apples and bananas in the old cliché. In economics, where guns and butter is the classical example given students, this is especially so because the field is so vast and the constituent components so varied. Some means to do this needed to be devised and so, over the centuries, money evolved as the answer.

Simplistically money provides both those two things, whilst also being the medium of exchange. In turn accounting evolved as the means for recording and tracking transactions, both for the commercial organisations that are the primary vehicles for trading and for the economies in which they operate. As a result, however, it has somewhat blurred the lines between commerce and economics, not least because the macro level accounting is not necessarily the aggregation of the micro-level and nor is it subject to the same rules.

Accounting systems are simply the means of recording financial transactions. For commercial activity they have developed the sophistication necessary to integrate profit into the transactions themselves. They thus appear to be able to handle the concept without difficulty but, as we saw earlier, cannot be totally relied upon, especially if the costs are not properly identified. Unfortunately "commercial cost" has historically been more narrowly defined than "economic cost". It is thus susceptible to being understated. Sadly there are a number of forces that act together to compound the likelihood of this, and they do not have any obvious counter-balances.

Remember, the smaller the cost the bigger the profit, thus:

- The overwhelming commercial incentive on the part of the seller to maximise profit inevitably reduces the imperative to properly identify all the hidden, indirect costs.

- All other things being equal, the lower sellers think their costs, the lower the price they will ask the prospective buyer. So there is little likelihood of the latter pointing out any understating of costs to the seller, because of the self-same motive.

In order to get the costs right it is imperative to get closer to the economic cost and that requires both the action and reaction to be included. In other words the cost of tree-felling in the rain forest should not be confined only to the consumable costs incurred in cutting and shipping the trees; or the cost of mining to the extraction costs, etc. Of course this is becoming increasingly apparent, but proper understanding and application of Newton's Law should have made us aware of this long before now.

The most glaring conclusion from a better understanding of Newton's Law and its wider implication has to be that there is scientifically no such thing as profit.

Factoring profit into the equation distorts the purity of the natural law identified by Newton, as well as the very basics of pure economics. Pure economics ultimately deals with humankind's utilisation of resources and so it is very closely aligned with natural science and thus subject to the same fundamental laws. Every action or transaction thus has an equal and opposite action or transaction, and so the whole balancing system is fundamentally the same as the one for the chemical element table. The failure to understand this means, for at least two or three hundred years, commercial success has been measured on the wrong basis and profits have been false. The price we will now have to pay for global warming is simply picking up the bill for the earlier unidentified costs.

It is almost certain that we would not have consumed resources on the same scale or at the same rate if we had recognised the full costs and adjusted the prices accordingly. The price then would likely have become too great for a buyer to be found willing to meet it. Unfortunately, it is this and future generations that will now have to pay the price, both economically and in a standard of living considerably lower than that which we might otherwise have anticipated or even to which we have become accustomed.

THE TITANIC ICEBERG

When I first started writing this, it was at this point that I started looking at the possible objections to these ideas and what was necessary to make my case stronger. The sudden dramatic downturn in the global economy has however, done the job for me and, hopefully, saved me from the traditional defence of shooting the messenger. Let's look at two specific examples now that prove the point beyond possible contradiction.

THE FINANCIAL MARKETS

The US government has spent close to $1 trillion, if not more, to rescue financial institutions that otherwise would have failed. I have no way of knowing or measuring the reported profits of these organisations over their respective lifetimes, but I would hazard a guess that the "bailout" is likely to be greater than their accumulated tax payments. Even if I am wrong the scale of the figures involved significantly reduces the average profits of the respective institutions for decades, thus proving that their accounting has been questionable at best, and downright false at worst. The problem is not just confined to the US either. There have been reports that the equivalent bailout in Europe will total 5.5 trillion euros or more than 5 times the cost of the Second World War. (And to put that in perspective, it was only in late 2007 or early 2008 that Britain paid the final instalment on her war loans!)

THE MOTOR INDUSTRY

The US motor industry has also been seeking a $15 billion bailout from the US government in order to survive. The motor industry is a bell-weather for economic performance and if there is any industry that knows the highs and lows of cyclical business this is it. Consequently, the inability of the industry leaders to run their businesses well enough to survive the current economic crunch suggests that they too have not had any idea of their true costs.

These events were avoidable and to that extent equivalent to the Titanic hitting the iceberg. No matter how unsinkable a ship is supposed to be, it will always be likely to sink if it is driven at close to full speed into an iceberg. And there will always be icebergs (or at least until the polar icecaps melt completely!) Similarly, there will always be the risk of commercial failure in business. If, however, the chances are to be reduced it is vital that the costs are properly and fully identified. These instances confirm my argument that this is not being done.

Perhaps the theory of evolution is true after all – and our ancestors were frogs, not monkeys! Joking aside, the water is certainly getting considerably hotter and we need to do something, quickly.

THE IMPLICATIONS

It would seem that "the loony left" may have been right all along and that profit has been given too much weight and influence, and infiltrated all aspects of economic and social life with potentially disastrous results. Certainly it seems that in the bi-polar world of capitalism and socialism, socialism, has become the victor.

Government intervention and the scale of that intervention reinforce my earlier point about the increasing centralisation of power. For starters these rescue initiatives have, in one fell swoop, converted the world's largest capitalist economy into the world's largest socialist one overnight. The implications of this are profound, because they suggest the complete failure of capitalism. The extent to which it has happened and the ease with which it did also reinforces my argument that the boundaries are more blurred than any staunch supporter of either faction would like to believe. Perhaps, more than anything, this reinforces Joan Robinson's theory.

However, this is more than an ideological issue, for the concept of profit is ultimately integral to both and the method of measuring it still needs to be resolved.

A SECOND LOOK AT NEWTON

Capitalism has seen a generally higher standard of living for the greater majority than any other system yet conceived. The big question that appears to hang over it now is whether it was just the macro-economic equivalent of pyramid selling. Has the bubble now well and truly burst, or does it have enough redeeming features to form the basis for a new ideology that will see us through the current difficulties?

If we are to avoid the risk of being guilty of superficial thinking and looking for solutions to symptoms rather than systemic solutions we need to ensure that we are not giving Newton's Law too much credence. After all it is only Newton's 3rd Law of *Motion*, which, if you missed the implications of the italics, tells us two things:

1. It cannot be too important, otherwise it would be number one; and

2. That it has a very limited field of application.

Thus there is a very real possibility that the expanded role ascribed to it here is a scientific stretch, and certainly one that has not been empirically proven. Furthermore, it can even be said that it has been used to give credence to an argument of logic and not of science, and as such the attempt is idiomatic rather than precise. This makes it important to ensure that the conclusions reached are not exaggerated or incredible, even though the current climate supports the case.

The difficulty in drawing conclusions here is that one is attempting to cross disciplinary boundaries, for Newton's Law is physical science, while economics is social science. To find any common ground thus necessitates looking at things from a completely different perspective. Let's start by shifting the focus onto economics.

As you likely know the word economy is derived from the Greek "Oikonomia" which in turn stems from the word "oikos" meaning house. This word also provides the root of the words "ecology" – which Webster's Dictionary[8] defines as, "1. *The branch of biology that deals with the relationship between living organisms and their environment. 2. In sociology, the relationship between the distribution of human groups with reference to material resources, and the consequent social and cultural patterns*" – and "ecosystem" which the same source defines as, "*A system made up of a of a community of animals, plants, and bacteria and its inter-related physical and chemical environments.*"

The relevance of these different definitions is that an ecosystem is generally considered to be perfectly balanced and self-sustaining; capable of indefinite survival so long as this balance is not disturbed. If you disturb that balance the whole ecology is threatened and faces complete disaster and destruction – which is precisely what is happening with the

---

[8] Webster New Twentieth Century Dictionary – Simon and Schuster 1979

threat of global warming. In its purest sense, economy could be considered to be the social ecosystem. However, the push for profit is a completely alien concept in any self-regulating, self-balancing environment and so we start to see that the earlier conclusions may be valid.

While "economics" fundamentally means "the management of the household", one of the definitions of the "science" of economics is "the management of scarce resources". This deals with the laws of supply and demand. It implies a starting point of lack, which is an immediate departure from the balance we have just been considering, and a perspective that inevitably starts to corrupt the entire system.

A key feature of economics is its subdivision into microeconomics – which deals with the small scale, individual, household or small business aspects of the field – and macroeconomics, which deals with the management of resources at a national or international level. These are obviously inextricably interconnected but are two very different disciplines. It can be dangerous to assume what applies at the lower level automatically also apply at the higher.

The illustration earlier, equating Newton's Law with the universal table of elements is analogous to a macroeconomic perspective. In the big picture everything does remain in balance, but "on the ground" the balance may be more difficult to identify, and its effects remain unseen. Going back to the example of the potassium turning into oxygen, its all very well saying that the potassium has turned into oxygen and so the balance remains, but there is no known way to turn the oxygen back into potassium (or if there is, we certainly weren't told about it. And there certainly is no known way to turn all the carbon dioxide back to fossil fuel to reverse the trend towards global warming.) Consequently, in an economy where potassium is important, the change is undesirable: its use can create a chronic shortage in supply and upset the whole balance of the system and place it in jeopardy.

So the links between Newton's Law and economics and the malevolent effects of profits can be justified. The heart of the issue is the divorce of "business" and "economics." The science of business has become too far removed from the science of economics and the dichotomy is dangerous and definitely damaging.

Unfortunately being "right" doesn't actually do anything to solve the problem. Removing the concept of profit from business is anathema to any but the most ardent socialist and, as we have already seen, they haven't yet come up with any feasible or viable alternative.

LOSS OF SPIRIT

It is evident, however, that we are going to have to invest far more effort in identifying the true costs of things, in order that the "super-profits" of the past are avoided. With "environmental repair" costs already looming large on the horizon, we cannot afford to load future generations with additional costs arising from industry bailouts like those we have seen in the financial services and motor industry.

The current situation makes it easy to become pessimistic, but there is no need to give in to despair or become despondent. Human history is a story of progress and, despite a rocky road and some undoubtedly dark periods in which we have hardly covered ourselves in glory as a species, ultimately we have always been able to meet and rise above the challenges presented and there is no reason to doubt it can happen again. Roosevelt's words, *"We have nothing to fear but fear itself",* have become something of a cliché, but they still resonate with a basic truth. The fact is, *"There is a spirit in man"* (The Bible, Job 32:8) and when we find that spirit we overcome fear and find the resources we need.

Unfortunately, starting from a premise of lack is not the way to go about finding it. And that is where economics begins, and is also where it finds some commonality with the "hard sciences". Of course all earthly thinking is ultimately coloured by limitation and lack; deterioration and decay. To some extent it has to be, because it is dominated by physical matter, and material resources are finite. This sense of ultimate limitation is epitomised by the fact we even have forecasts predicting when the sun is going to cool and earth become a "dead" planet. Such thinking is literally dispiriting, because it actually ignores the "spiritual" aspect completely. And the spiritual is vitally important.

To understand why, it is perhaps a good idea to put things in context and explain what I mean by "spiritual".

If you are hungry and have a single apple and eat it, then the apple is gone and you are faced with starvation unless you can find a further supply of apples or other food. If you give the apple to your friend who is even hungrier and he eats it, then you have done something that makes you feel good and him feel less hungry, but the apple has still gone: you remain hungry and neither of your prospects have improved. However, if you are feeling depressed and observe something amusing that makes you laugh you feel better. If you then share that experience with your friend, repeating the story will make you both laugh and you will both feel better. The difference is that the apple is matter and therefore can only be consumed once, and its goodness only experienced once. The joke, however, is not material but "spiritual" and therefore can be shared over and over and the good multiplied. And that's the difference: the former is finite while the latter is infinite.

THE IMPORTANCE OF THE SPIRITUAL

So why is the spiritual important? Quite simply because it is the only true multiplier, and consequently, the more we can isolate and build on it in our lives, the better off we will be. It is commonly accepted that the team with the greater "team spirit" will often outperform a superior team and spirit is the David and Goliath phenomenon that we need to find more of, if we are to find answers.

Over-emphasis of the material at the expense of the spiritual is literally "dis-spiriting". That is why, at a period in human history when we have accumulated more material possessions, have more labour saving tools and more leisure time than ever before, we are also arguably the most dissatisfied generation in history. Suicide is the ultimate statement of dissatisfaction and despair, and suicide rates certainly bear this out as a growing proportion of the population resorts to it. If that is not evidence enough, never before has the world reached such a low that apparently intelligent people are willing to go out and kill and maim as many people as they possibly can in effecting their own suicide. If this is not a sign of rising water temperatures and a need to take a fresh look at our way of life and see what needs to be changed, nothing is.

Of course this is not saying that the answer to the world's problems is to tell more jokes! The point is quite simply that the economic measures we have been using to date have had serious shortcomings that have perhaps never been recognised, and that one of the consequences of this has been to contribute to a generally declining sense of worth. A practical alternative has to be found to profit as a measure of commercial performance. This is perhaps easier said than done and certainly presents a massive challenge, but there are unquestionably issues that need to be addressed and new ideas are needed.

THE VALUE MOTIVE

The best solution that I have come across is promoted by Paul Kearns in his book, "The Value Motive: The ONLY Alternative to the Profit Motive"[9]. In some ways this is part of the book that I wanted to write, but Kearns has said it all so much better than I could, and has more relevant experience and expertise to do the subject far more justice than I ever could. I therefore heartily recommend it to anyone who is looking for alternatives and a better way to manage society.

In his introduction, Kearns writes, *"This book has a single, very simple message. Manage for maximum value."* Clearly, that has to be the answer for a world that is hard-pressed to optimise the way in which it uses its economic resources, and, in a nutshell, sums up one of the key messages of this book too, for as he adds, *"At the root of this debate, the total package, are the political and economic systems that we choose to run society."* (His emphasis not mine!) This, of course, means *"a motive that simultaneously enriches society materially and spiritually."*

One of the key points that Kearns makes is that *"all organisations should be defined by what outputs they are meant to achieve and judged on what scarce resources they use up in achieving these outputs."* Of course the immediate implication of this is that there is then no conceptual difference between for-profit, non-profit and public sectors organisations - something that I have believed for a very long time.

I hope, over the course of this book, to reinforce that point, and to start giving some answers to the leading question of "Who should ultimately decide how resources are allocated?"

---

[9] The Value Motive: The ONLY Alternative to the Profit Motive. (Wiley & Sons © 2007)

CHAPTER SIX

Compounding The Problem

"The power of tax is the power to destroy."

JOHN MARSHALL

Governments generate a significant proportion of their revenue from corporation taxes, based on profits. So if the calculation of profits is dubious, the potential consequences for governments are enormous, no matter what the nature of the political system. This may not be immediately apparent as the false accounting depicted actually seems to benefit government, at least in the short term, since it effectively earns more revenue from the overstated profits. This, however, ignores the economic inefficiencies already highlighted, as well as the costs of the industry bailouts recently witnessed and the potential for more in the future.

It is, however, the longer term implications that are daunting, for they clearly point to the likelihood of government revenue shrinking dramatically. This means there will be strong pressures to find alternative sources which will impact business and individuals alike. Never forget that government is predominantly a consumer and not a producer and so has little scope to generate revenue of its own accord, but has to rely on taxes and excises for the bulk of its revenue. This means that government pain is effectively our pain.

The only alternative is to borrow. Just as we have to borrow if we do not earn all we need, government can also borrow to make up a shortfall in revenue. Indeed this is a traditional source of funding for government. In the same way any amounts we borrow have to be paid for out of future income, so too does government borrowing. And just as the rate of interest we have to pay reflects both the required rate of return of the lender and the perceived risk of not being repaid, so does that of government.

Consequently, in an environment where revenues are diminishing there will inevitably be a concern about government's ability to repay. This means they will be required to pay considerably higher rates than they are currently. We have already seen the detrimental effects of debt, but these are exacerbated by high interest rates. As a result government borrowing will either further reduce national economic wealth or governments will reduce or eliminate their borrowing. This will increase the importance of revenue generation from taxes and excises.

It is therefore vital that we have efficient tax systems. Anything less will enhance the ability of tax to destroy and make the quote above a prophecy rather than an observation. Unfortunately, our tax systems are anything but efficient and this has to be rectified if we are to meet the challenges ahead.

THE FUNDAMENTAL FLAW OF CORPORATION TAX

There is an even more fundamental flaw tied to using profit as a basis for calculating a business' tax liability than the reliability of the method of determining profit, and that is the logic of using profit in the first place. After all *taxing on the basis of profit effectively means that government is subsidising the inefficient!*

Amazingly this is something that nobody ever seems to have recognised or challenged, but just think about it. Businessmen in any economy, capitalist or socialist, work to maximise profit, which simply means doing everything possible to maximise sales and reduce costs. The bigger the profit the more successful a business is considered. And, all other things being equal, the greater the profit, the more tax the business pays. (Thus, theoretically at least, it can validly be claimed that an alternative measure of success is the amount of tax paid, although, for reasons identified later, businessmen would not consider this to be a reasonable measure!)

Other companies may compete in the same market, offering exactly the same services but not making equivalent profits. Why not? Quite simply, because their managers are not as efficient i.e. they cannot generate the same sales or reduce costs to the same level. As a result these companies are not required to pay as much tax. Yet they are using the same natural and economic resources. Consequently, when looked at from a macro-economic perspective where the overall objective is to ensure the efficient use of scarce resources, it is quite clear that the more successful business is being penalised for its success. The natural corollary to this is that the inefficient business is benefiting from being inefficient and thus could be said to be subsidised.

This logic is irrefutable as long as tax is calculated on the basis of absolute profit amounts. It shows the enormous gap between micro and macro-economic theory and the lack of "joined-up thinking" in economic management. This means that, nationally, economic resources are not optimised, or, to put it another way, are partly wasted. And, as we saw in Chapter 4, waste has a cost, whether or not it is recognised. Consequently there is a responsibility to better recognise this waste and ensure that it is eliminated and/or the associated costs properly recognised.

OTHER FLAWS IN THE TAX SYSTEM

Nor is this the only problem with tax regimes. Most western countries have a number of other inherent flaws in their systems that are unrecognised or ignored.

Instrument of Policy

From the beginning, tax systems have been a mechanism for redistributing wealth, providing the means for society to safeguard the interests of the poor and help create an environment in which poverty was not hereditary, and where all have the opportunity to better themselves and for "the pursuit of happiness". There is nothing inherently wrong with this ambition. From prehistoric times the stronger of the human species has recognised an obligation to look after the weaker in their social order, and this is just a more technical way of doing so. As Franklin Roosevelt said, *"Taxes are the dues that we pay for the privileges of membership in an organised society."*

Unfortunately they create an intrinsic danger of political objectives taking precedence over sound economics. It should never be forgotten that the ultimate protection of the less fortunate lies in the ability of others to look out for them. This in turn requires their situation to be as strong and secure as possible. Looking after the less fortunate always entails a cost to others. Thus there comes a point at which that cost can become excessive and be to the detriment of the greater good of all. It is an extremely difficult call to identify precisely what that point would be, but, as indicated earlier, there is definitely a case for arguing that our welfare state has gone too far.

Whether one accepts this or not is irrelevant right now: the issue here is not the merits or otherwise of the welfare state or even its current condition, but simply that the debate only arises because the system is open to misuse. The argument as to whether it is abused is entirely subjective, but there would simply be no possibility if policy and national revenue collection were kept segregated. Using the tax system to drive policy, effectively distorts the market. It impairs the mechanics of the economy, and its ability to govern economic efficiency when left to itself. After all, one of the fundamental economic principles is that it is impossible to achieve optimal economic efficiency when the market is tampered with.

Policy Distortion

The main issue with using tax as a policy vehicle is that it is the primary means used by an incoming government to undo the policies of its predecessor with which it disagrees. This puts it at the forefront of "political creep" and, rather like that old master described earlier, it gets distorted as each year a layer of new features is added, whilst others are removed. This political "tacking" undermines economic consistency. It engenders a risk of "contradictory consequences", where a change intended to achieve one objective actually undermines the ability to deliver a previous, equally important policy objective.

Unnecessary Complication

However, another by-product of this tendency is the degree of complexity that gets built into the system. The accumulation of new initiatives to increase government revenue, combined with the drive to meet political ends, makes tax law increasingly complex. Even Albert Einstein is said to have lamented that, *"The hardest thing in the world to understand is the income tax"*, and that was before tax law ran into volumes of thousands of pages. If he thought that, what chance do the rest of us have?

A recent newspaper report seems to bear this out. It states that, according to the National Audit Office £157 million of tax was overpaid last year due to processing errors by HM Revenue and Customs while £125 million was underpaid.[10] (Note who comes out on top overall – if you thought the dice was loaded against you it would appear that your suspicions were correct!) These errors affected 1.5 million taxpayers, but worse than the cost of the errors themselves, is the cost of identify and correcting them; both in terms of actual outlays and wasted time and effort.

---

[10] "Taxman's errors cost us millions." Manchester Evening News, 6 July, 2007

All that is in itself an indictment of the system, showing how unreasonably complex and unwieldy it has all become, but the fact that tax law has generated a whole industry of its own should clinch the argument. Barbara Ehrenreich's humorous statement, *"It seems to me that there must be an ecological limit to the number of paper pushers the earth can sustain, and human civilisation will collapse when the number of, say tax lawyers, exceeds the world's total population of farmers, weavers, fisherpersons and paediatric nurses"*, makes a very serious point. There is something seriously wrong when whole industries develop around tax and the ways to minimise paying it.

This is why, as suggested earlier, the amount of tax paid could not be an economic performance figure. The extent to which businesses reduce their tax bill is a distinct measure for both the businesses themselves and these parasitic industries that feed off the system. The economic waste of such a system is impossible to justify, and the amount of human intellectual capital taken up in activity which ultimately adds so little value to society and thus can be said to be fundamentally unproductive, is little short of criminal. It could and should be put to better use!

Burgeoning Bureaucracy

The growth of industries around tax is only one aspect of economic inefficiency. The complexity of the system inevitably also makes demands for a bigger civil service bureaucracy to collect and administer the system. This in turn increases the cost of collection. It would be interesting to ascertain the proportion of revenue governments spend in collecting taxes and their trends over the years. Governments themselves have recognised this and so tried to pass the burden of collection onto business itself, with initiatives like PAYE and VAT. Despite this delegation and the mitigating benefits of increasingly sophisticated computer systems, collections costs are likely to be higher than in the past, and certainly considerably higher than they would be if tax structures were kept simpler.

This burgeoning bureaucracy is itself fuelled by a combination of two things:

1. The high tax rates themselves; and

2. The ever widening net of taxes being levied.

Reaganomics and Thatcherism proved that reducing income tax rates stimulated economic growth. An unanticipated benefit, however, was the fact that tax revenues also actually increased, proving that the higher the tax burden the greater the lengths to which people would go to avoid paying taxes.

One would think it was a no-brainer: reduce taxes to a reasonable level and reduce their complexity and there would be no need for a whole industry of tax consultants and lawyers. Again the entire situation has been summed up more eloquently and more humorously by the American comedian Will Rogers who claimed, *"The income tax has made more liars out of Americans than golf. Even when you make a tax form out on the level, you don't know when it's through if you are a crook or a martyr"*. The ability to find humour in serious situations is undoubtedly one of humankind's most enduring and endearing qualities, but there is a satirical bite to this which does require us to do more than just laugh. One of the reasons for the high collection costs is the need to police the system because of the length to which people will go to "get away with" whatever they can.

Growth of Government

Reaganomics and Thatcherism, despite their good intentions, were not so successful at reducing the role of government in the economy. Whatever early success there might have been seems to have been short-lived and even subsequently reversed. There are any number of explanations for this and they could probably be the subject of a book on their own and so are beyond the scope of this one. Suffice to say that, while the degree of influence and the relative effects will vary between the US and the UK, they may well include:

- The election of New Labour in the UK, compounded by Tony Blair's tendency to want to be personally involved with everything.

- The failure of capitalism outlined earlier, with the increasing levels of dissatisfaction it brought as the emperor's clothes were found to be an illusion.

- The backlash against the rush to create personal wealth which appeared to have eroded time honoured methods of funding infrastructure growth, development and maintenance.

- The need to find other sources of revenue to meet the shortfall in what was needed to fund government, and the increasing influence of government in all sectors of the economy.

- 9/11 and its aftermath. People, stunned by the scale of unprecedented barbarism and hatred, turned initially to government for answers, while the costs of beefed up security in turn boosted the requirements of government.

As Rush Limbaugh so succinctly put it, *"No nation ever taxed itself to prosperity"*. Consequently these pressures for greater government influence must inevitably have a debilitating economic effect. Over recent decades the government share of GDP has increased in most economies. This ultimately has to effect their ability to grow and certainly impacts negatively on a country's economic competitiveness and hence on their ability to maintain their existing standard of living. This brings us back to the welfare state and its costs, because the demand for social benefits creates an inflationary cycle of government spending, perpetuating an increasingly vicious circle.

Total Tax Revenue as a Percentage of GDP (OECD, 2002)

Country	Tax as percentage of GDP
Japan	25.8
United States	26.4
Ireland	28.4
Switzerland	30.3
Australia	31.5
Canada	33.9
Spain	35.6
United Kingdom	35.8
United Kingdom (2008-2009)	38.3
Germany	36.0
Italy	42.6
France	44.0
Sweden	50.2
OECD Total	36.3
EU 15	36.3

Source: Reform Think Tank Website[11]

The above table explains why Ireland has been the fastest growing economy in Europe in recent years. The highlighted figures, showing that the UK proportion is expected to increase to 38.3% in 2008-2009 (a not insubstantial 6.9% increase), supports the argument about the cycle of government growth. While the UK proportion is comparatively low, this increase is still a concern. The demands for health care, transport, education, energy, defence, flood protection and pensions indicate such a strong upward pressure that this growth figure even appears conservative. This pressure inevitably begs the question as to what governments in the past were doing with tax revenues when rates were considerably higher, as well as why more wasn't made of the benefits of North Sea oil when the

---

[11] Reform is a centre right think tank that claims to be "determinedly independent and strictly non-party"

reserves made the UK a net exporter of energy? This reinforces the case that governments are not best placed to oversee economic efficiency.

With the chickens coming home to roost with such things as global warning, as well as the other issues highlighted here, particularly the aging demographics, it is self-evident that we have to rethink our whole approach.

In case you find that picture depressing the following gives a delightful, tongue in cheek, perspective into the extent to which government is increasingly involved in every day life.

IF NELSON WAS ALIVE TODAY

Nelson: "Order the signal, Hardy."

Hardy: "Aye, aye sir."

Nelson: "Hold on, that's not what I dictated to Flags. What's the meaning of this?"

Hardy: "Sorry sir?"

Nelson (reading aloud): "'England expects every person to do his or her duty, regardless of race, gender, sexual orientation, religious persuasion or disability.' - What gobbledegook is this?"

Hardy: "Admiralty policy, I'm afraid, sir. We're an equal opportunities employer now. We had the devil's own job getting 'England' past the censors, lest it be considered racist."

Nelson: "Gadzooks, Hardy. Hand me my pipe and tobacco."

Hardy: "Sorry sir. All naval vessels have now been designated smoke-free working environments."

Nelson: "In that case, break open the rum ration. Let us splice the mainbrace to steel the men before battle."

Hardy: "The rum ration has been abolished, Admiral. Its part of the Government's policy on binge drinking."

Nelson: "Good heavens, Hardy. I suppose we'd better get on with it. Full speed ahead."

Hardy: "I think you'll find that there's a 4 knot speed limit in this stretch of water."

Nelson: "Damn it man! We are on the eve of the greatest sea battle in history. We must advance with all dispatch. Report from the crow's nest please."

Hardy: "That won't be possible, sir."

Nelson: "What?"

Hardy: "Health and Safety have closed the crow's nest, sir. No harness; and they said that rope ladders don't meet regulations. They won't let anyone up there until a proper scaffolding can be erected."

Nelson: "Then get me the ship's carpenter without delay, Hardy."

Hardy: "He's busy knocking up a wheelchair access to the foredeck Admiral."

Nelson: "Wheelchair access? I've never heard anything so absurd."

Hardy: "Health and safety again, sir. We have to provide a barrier-free environment for the differently abled."

Nelson: "Differently abled? I've only one arm and one eye and I refuse even to hear mention of the word. I didn't rise to the rank of admiral by playing the disability card."

Hardy: "Actually, sir, you did. The Royal Navy is under represented in the areas of visual impairment and limb deficiency."

Nelson: "Whatever next? Give me full sail. The salt spray beckons."

Hardy: "A couple of problems there too, sir. Health and safety won't let the crew up the rigging without hard hats. And they don't want anyone breathing in too much salt - haven't you seen the adverts?"

Nelson: "I've never heard such infamy. Break out the cannon and tell the men to stand by to engage the enemy."

Hardy: "The men are a bit worried about shooting at anyone, Admiral."

Nelson: "What? This is mutiny!"

Hardy: "It's not that, sir. It's just that they're afraid of being charged with murder if they actually kill anyone. There's a couple of legal-aid lawyers on board, watching everyone like hawks."

Nelson: "Then how are we to sink the Frenchies and the Spanish?"

Hardy: "Actually, sir, we're not."

Nelson: "We're not?"

Hardy: "No, sir. The French and the Spanish are our European partners now. According to the Common Fisheries Policy, we shouldn't even be in this stretch of water. We could get hit with a claim for compensation."

Nelson: "But you must hate a Frenchman as you hate the devil."

Hardy: "I wouldn't let the ship's diversity co-ordinator hear you saying that sir. You'll be up on disciplinary report."

Nelson: "You must consider every man an enemy, who speaks ill of your King."

Hardy: "Not any more, sir. We must be inclusive in this multicultural age. Now put on your Kevlar vest; it's the rules. It could save your life!"

Nelson: "Don't tell me - health and safety. Whatever happened to rum, sodomy and the lash?"

Hardy: As I explained, sir, rum is off the menu! And there's a ban on corporal punishment."

Nelson: "What about sodomy?"

Hardy: "I believe that is now legal, sir."

Nelson: "In that case... kiss me, Hardy."

Loss of Social Conscience

The growth in government and the part it plays in our everyday lives has other less recognised consequences. One is that we tend to become less personally independent as we come to depend on government more. Some commentators support this by maintaining that society is increasingly inclined to blame government when thing go wrong or to look to it to provide solutions when any new problem arises. It is unclear whether there is any empirical evidence to support such claims, but it certainly would be a natural corollary to the lack of accountability identified as an issue earlier in the book. There does, however, seem to be more tangible evidence to support claims that individual charitable giving diminishes in societies where government plays a bigger part in the economy. Of course this is entirely logical because the greater the share of private income a government secures through taxation, the less discretionary income people have at their disposal.

However, there may be another reason too: namely that the more of our income that government absorbs the more we expect it to provide for those less fortunate than we are. There have been many commentaries bemoaning the selfish nature of modern western society, but it is entirely possible that increasing government "interference" in the economy and providing for welfare has exacerbated this, by creating a sense of "that's what we pay taxes for" and so leaving us with the idea that we are absolved from any personal responsibility. *"When confronted with American largesse [charitable giving], the British tend to fall back on three face-savers: they're richer than us; they get more generous tax breaks; and they're social climbing. There is some truth in all of these, but they don't go the whole way to explaining why Americans give about three times more to charity, as a proportion of GDP, than we do",* Camilla Cavendish: The Times 22nd June, 2006. The fact is that Americans across the income spectrum are more generous, possibly because its social history has made the UK less inclined to charitable giving, but almost certainly because they do not have a social network and are therefore more inclined to be grateful for good fortune and so, in a spirit of "there but for the grace of God go I" likely to help those they consider less fortunate.

Once again it is not the degree of validity or otherwise of this theory that matters, but the principle itself. The proportion of GDP represented by taxation must inevitably have a bearing on both our ability and our willingness to help others.

The ability to feel good about ourselves is a primary factor in the human psyche. Unfortunately, the extent to which we are either unwilling or unable to help others must inevitably have a deleterious affect on our own sense of self and, consequently, on our quality of life and well-being. It could well be that our welfare state ultimately erodes the self-worth of recipient and non-recipient alike. Hence there is actually more truth than humour in Arthur Godfrey's words, *"I am proud of paying taxes. The only thing is I could be just as proud for half the money."*

CHAPTER SEVEN

The Consequences

"The tax collector must love poor people.
He is creating so many of them."

BILL VAUGHAN

There is certainly good reason to rue the manner in which government spends our taxes! Furthermore a look at the demands that government is facing and the pressures to increase its revenue grab are hardly encouraging and are enough to drive one to despair. As we saw earlier, UK tax revenues amount to 35.8% of GDP, and are set to rise to 38.3% for 2008-9 but the demands being made on government mean that the likelihood is that it could be even higher.[12] Most of the challenges facing the country have already been touched on, but let's take a closer look at these to see why this is.

HEALTHCARE

Hardly a day goes by when this subject doesn't make the news. The Labour government has poured billions into the NHS over the past few years and while they can justifiably claim that it will take time for the effects to be evidenced, the fact remains that many insiders are sceptical about the manner in which the money has been spent and the likelihood of seeing the promised benefits. Patient waiting times – the

---

[12] These figures were all forecasts prior to the downturn in the economy. What effect the downturn will have has not been considered here. Nevertheless, Government's role in bailing out the financial sector and trying to stimulate the economy is going to have a significant impact on these figures in the longer-term – an issue that is currently the subject of much political debate.

performance measure targeted when Labour was first elected – have reduced to lower-than-target levels, but problems with hygiene and the superbug MRSA in particular, continue to be a major concern, as does the time-bomb of caring for the aging baby-boomer population.

This also remains a potentially significant problem for the rest of Europe and the US in light of the changing demographics and the aging population.

PENSIONS

Needless to say the aging population and the need to meet a growing pension liability from a shrinking revenue base yielded by a proportionately smaller workforce is also a major cause for concern. This will unquestionably drain resources and prevent expenditure on other important priorities. Once again this is a universal problem in most developed nations.

DEFENCE

Reference has already been made to the consequences of 9/11 and I doubt they really need further explanation. By far the biggest is the cost to the Exchequer of the additional security measures resulting from the need for more active intelligence and homeland security. Even if there were to be no more attacks, the ongoing terrorist threat simply demands the devotion of resources on a hitherto unprecedented scale. Helping other nations like Bali and India deal with their attacks creates further demands on intelligence and military resources.

This situation is compounded by the ongoing wars in Afghanistan and Iraq, while other peacekeeping duties add to the demands. Ironically, in the face of such demands, British military personnel are fighting with inappropriate, outdated and sub-standard equipment and the forces are being heavily criticised for the earlier cut-backs and poor planning which have put lives at unnecessary risk. Consequently further expenditure is required and will likely continue even if the present non-intelligence commitments are scaled back. Indeed one cannot help wondering if the scheduled British withdrawal from Iraq in June 2009 is due more to the inability to continue on the present basis than "having completed our mission" as claimed. In any event, the withdrawal is going to create a further strain on the US economy at a time where they are also experiencing unprecedented demands on fiscal expenditure and will struggle to meet their commitments.

EDUCATION

Education is possibly the field that most needs a fresh approach. As the world gets more and more sophisticated and complex, the approach to education remains largely rooted in the past. I made reference earlier to the school performance tables that dominate school selection here in the UK. Can there be anything more depressing and distressing for any parent than to know that circumstances dictate that they cannot do any better for their children than send them to the local "bottom-of-the-table" comprehensive?

The term lifelong learning is bandied about in educational circles, and yet there seems to be so little cohesive action to enable it. There seems to be no correlation between "learning" and "self-advancement". The traditional perspective of learning as drumming things into young people seems to be as dominant today as it was in the early twentieth century. The focus is almost exclusively on "passing" tests within pre-determined time limits and at regular intervals. Those whose abilities match this pre-determined time-frame remain virtually anonymous. Those whose do not correspond exactly are made to feel stupid and worthless, while those whose abilities exceed these expectations are held back to wait for those whose don't whilst they lose any discipline or the will to press on to new challenges.

The quantity of what "needs" to be learned continues to grow, while the time-frame for teaching remains finite, and consequently the depth of coverage gets less and less until the subject matter itself becomes increasingly worthless. Do you doubt this? Then ask why it is that the first year at university is no longer part of a degree course? The government in its wisdom has decreed that more people need to go to university (and get into debt to do so) but the first year actually doesn't count. It is a 'foundation' year so that those who really aren't equipped and shouldn't be there get 'weeded out' while the rest are brought up to a level that equips them to cope with what they will be doing in the following years.

The net effect of all this is that exam results show year on year improvements, while students complete a modern 3 year degree in what is actually only two academic years. And the general public is expected to believe that this is because standards are improving!

The tragedy of all this is the downward spiral it creates. Fewer and fewer people opt for teaching as a career. Those that do are no longer the ones with the aptitude or the vocation but those who see it as a way to earn a decent salary with plenty of paid holidays. It becomes simply a job just like any other, with the performance measure being the ability to get "passes". This is achieved by marking course work in draft form so that the final work looks to be of a higher standard than what was actually produced, and doing so many past papers that by the time the exams come the students will likely already have done the exact question they get in their paper and will hopefully be smart enough to recognise it. The best teachers are no longer those who care for their pupils but those who play the system. Inevitably this demoralises and demotivates the good teachers, who then leave.

All in all it is a system that fosters mediocrity. It becomes a process where:

- The individuality is knocked out of the pupils and the average pupils become stars and those at either end of the spectrum are fortunate to avoid delinquency.

- There is a downward spiral in the quality of teachers as the good ones move on to be replaced by the less capable.

- Respect on both sides is non-existent: teachers have no respect for their students and the students have no respect for their teachers.

This is evidenced by the fact that in Britain *"fewer than half of teenagers finished compulsory schooling with five good GCSE's including maths and English and Ofsted (the governing body) reports that 1.5m pupils attend schools with substandard teaching and discipline."*[13] This is the educational equivalent of banks lending money to people who cannot afford to repay the loans, and it is a social and economic time bomb.

I cannot remember where, but I recently heard of a university professor who gets exceptional results from all his students and whose classes are oversubscribed many times over. He simply tells his students on their first day that they are all 'A' grade students and will all get 'A's if they just do what is required of them. So they do and they do. What we really need to do is make our young people feel that they are all 'A' grade students and not bombard them with tests and measures that prove otherwise and stop them feeling good about themselves.

This may seem to contradict the earlier point about lowering standards. It doesn't really. The difference is that here we are talking about constructively building students up rather than

---

[13] "Well, we did pay Matthews to keep having children" Sunday Times, 7 December, 2008

artificially doing so, which is the equivalent of printing money as you need it and ultimately watching it become worthless as inflation takes it toll. As someone once said "50% of all doctors finish in the bottom half of their class!" However, nobody ever asks their doctor which half of the class they finished in; they simply have the confidence that they are qualified to provide whatever treatment is necessary. Somehow we seem to regard them as all 'A' grade. That is a simple consequence of faith in the medical training they receive, but will only last as long as we have that faith. We need to have the same confidence in our education system, and more importantly so do our children. They need a system that will make them confident, competent adults, properly equipped to live up to their full potential. If we don't provide this, our medical training standards will also ultimately fail.

WELFARE

This is another subject that I have touched on earlier and another area where the system has been buried in good intentions. It is also the epitome of political correctness and so much of what is wrong with central government and its efforts to redistribute wealth. Instead of assisting people to better themselves and truly helping those that need help it has become a vehicle for the lazy and the crafty to exploit the system.

Lest you think this is simply bitter rambling on the part of a grumpy middle-aged man, let me quote from a recent report in the Sunday Times.[14] *"A mother with four children has been placed by her council in a £2m townhouse at the cost to the taxpayer of £91,000 a year. ... It costs £1,755 a week to rent – a bill met by housing benefit – and has a front and back garden, five bedrooms, two bathrooms, a double reception room and a roof terrace ... They are there with the approval*

---

[14] "Council pays out £90,000 a year in rent to a mother of four" Sunday Times 21 December, 2008

of both the local authority and the government. The property was picked out by the Royal Borough of Kensington and Chelsea, while the housing benefit payout was authorised by the Department for Work and Pensions (DWP). Neither apparently is to blame. The council says onerous government legislation is at fault forcing it to rehouse homeless council tenants within the borough. The DWP points finger firmly at the council for failing to look hard enough for alternative properties. Between them, however, they are presiding over a perverse benefits system that rewards the unemployed with the kind of properties that most taxpayers can only dream about. It is far from an isolated case. In Kensington and Chelsea alone there is an even more expensive property costing taxpayers £1,875 a week." The DWP argument seems to have some justification, because the report adds later, *"Cheaper accommodation is readily available at present, with a* **cursory search** *(my emphasis) showing similar five-bedroom property within the borough three miles away, available for £875 a week, half the price."*

A table included in the article based on information obtained under the Freedom of Information Act, shows the top monthly payments by councils, with the top 5 paying rental equivalents to £50,000 a year or more.

Housing Benefit

Top monthly payment in each council

1	Ealing	£12,458
2	Kensington & Chelsea	£8,125
3	Westminster	£5,200
4	Barnet	£5,158
5	Wandsworth	£4,193
6	Hackney	£3,900
7	Exeter	£3,619
8	Islington	£3,180
9	Slough	£2,722
10	Lambeth	£2,600

So you see I am not making it up, though you might be forgiven for thinking I had.

Unfortunately, that is not the end of the bad news. A further article on the same page is headlined "Welfare booms under Labour" and states, *"The number of people who have been on benefits for more than five years has increased nearly 30% under Labour, writes Steven Swinford. Official statistics show that since 1999 the number of long-term claimants has grown from 1.84m to 2.34m, a 27% rise, despite a fall in the overall number of those claiming from 5.4m to 5.1m. The increase has taken place despite Labour's pledge when it came to power in 1997 to make cutting benefit dependency a priority."*

Depressing though these figure are, they are doubly so if you factor in the fact that this all occurred during the longest economic boom in history! What is the prognosis now that we are officially entering recession? If this doesn't point to the water getting unbearably hot, I don't know what does. Yet even then, they are only the tip of the iceberg.

WELFARE, THE SOCIAL UNDERCLASS & CRIME

The benefit system has led to a second generation of benefit claimants. We now see a new generation of people who expect something for nothing, and who have no understanding of the work ethic and what it means to be independent or self-sufficient. This is a dangerous situation and needs to be nipped in the bud before we see a decline that makes the collapse of the Roman Empire look positively benign.

Let us take a specific example. Reporting on the conviction of a mother for kidnapping her own 9 year-old daughter, a newspaper editorial comment reported[15] *"This case is important, not because of what she did, horrible though that was, but what she exposed. She opened our eyes to an*

---

[15] "Well, we did pay Matthews to keep having children" Sunday Times, 7 December, 2008

underclass that most of us ignored or hoped would just go away. Matthews is the mother of seven children by five different men. She has never worked, but lived off benefits of £286.60 a week. The Matthews house was filthy. A neighbour declared, 'I wouldn't want to keep a pet dog in there, let alone children.' Her relationships with men were so promiscuous that when police built up a family tree it stretched to 300 names. Karen's nine-year-old daughter was regularly drugged to keep her quiet, had feet encrusted with dirt, was infested with head lice and flinched at any sudden noise. Police found a note scribbled by Shannon to her brother, 'Do you think we will get any tea tonight? If we're quiet we might get a bag of sweets. Don't talk too loud or get a beating.' This was a family receiving benefits of more than £20,000 a year before tax.[16] Seven children were going hungry to bed, not because of social deprivation but because their mother could not be bothered to feed them."

This is in the 21st century! However, shocking though this is it is not all. The report continues, *"The Matthews house is not a one-off. Researching a report on the care system, I met many children from families such as the Matthewses – including teenagers so starved and abused that it had stunted their growth. One boy recalled taking speed each morning 'just to get me to school'. Another had been given nothing to eat but dry cornflakes for three days. A third was told by her mother on her 13th birthday, 'Go out and sell your body. I am not feeding you any more.'"*

So who is to blame for the suffering of these children? These are obviously extreme examples and I am by no means trying to suggest that all welfare recipients treat their children like this. Nor do I want to fall into the trap of doing the very thing I am decrying – formulating policy on symptoms or issues rather than

---

[16] And probably living rent free in council provided housing on top of that.

principles. I am simply using these as examples to show that there is a problem and one that if not dealt with will grow. This is clearly a serious subject and one that needs to be addressed.

The article, however, does make a couple of additional key points.

Karen Matthews herself was one of seven children in and out of care.

It quotes Sir Norman Bettison, Chief Constable of the West Yorkshire Police as saying, *"We are talking here about the perverting influence of welfare. The more kids you have the more money you get."* If that is the case (and it *is* precisely what I am arguing) then the conclusion is totally valid that *"to accuse these young girls of being feckless is unjust. They understand and are simply responding to the economics of the situation."*

The moral breakdown and its implications are so depressing that they call for a little British humour to lighten the mood. So…

When Madonna married Guy Ritchie she said she liked the British and wanted to become just like them. Ironically, with her divorce she has succeeded: she is now a single mother with several kids, all by a different father.

Okay, back to more serious matters. The issue here is clearly one of the creation of an underclass, something that was highlighted by another high-profile criminal case: the shooting of 11 year-old Rhys Jones on his way home from football practice. Here too the case is important, not just because of the horror of what happened, but what it exposed, and the extent to which gang loyalty overrode any sense of morality, decency or remorse. Rhys was shot by a gang member shooting at a member of a rival gang. After the incident, the whole gang community closed ranks and abetted the perpetrator in his efforts to get away with murder, with the result that the police ended up charging a further 6 people as co-conspirators and for obstructing justice.

This ethos is behind the spate of teenage stabbings around the country and is helping turn the welfare state into a feral state. The latest statistics reveal that in the UK 5 people a week are being stabbed to death. Youngsters are growing up with an inferior education, no respect for the law, little or no sense of being loved, valued or appreciated and so they inevitably seek their own substitutes. In a pre-recession society where they have seen so much wealth and it has all seemed so remote it is inevitable that they will want a share. For many, with none of the usual brakes to persuade them otherwise, crime appears the only way to achieve it. Gang membership thus provides a double benefit: it gives them both a sense of belonging with a credibility that they would not otherwise have and a route to get their share of what everyone else has. In a recessionary world the economic pressures will simply be greater.

It is ironic, to say the least, that a government that campaigned under the slogan, "Tough on crime and tough on the causes of crime" has not been able to see that its own welfare regime may be one of the biggest causes of crime!

PRISONS AND POLICING

One needs to remember too, that this is happening in a country where the prison population is at an all-time high and the lack of prison space reached crisis-point. This creates a double whammy, with a need to spend more on both policing and criminal custody.

It has also resulted in the early release of a number of convicts and reluctance on the part of magistrates and judges to pass custodial sentences where they feel these can be avoided. This in turn affects the morale of police, by adding a sense of futility to their efforts, when (like many other public sector workers) they already feel:

- Underpaid for the work they do,

- The bureaucracy and paperwork reduces their actual police work,

- Priorities are misdirected by government target-setting and performance measurements.

TRANSPORT

Travelling in and around Britain is becoming increasingly fraught. The government faces a classic dilemma of trying to encourage more people to use public transport but the facilities and infrastructure do not further such ambitions.

Privatisation of the rail services has certainly bolstered the government coffers but any resulting benefits for passengers are becoming less and less obvious. The infrastructure is creaking and the routing of services is, I am told by people in the industry, more or less as it was in the worst days of British Rail, planned around the operators' rather than commuters' needs. The train companies put on a show of offering customer service but are still ultimately virtual monopolies with no direct competition over the routes they run. Fares continue to rise at above inflationary levels and are justified by the need to spend more on infrastructure to improve future service. However, the need to earn profits and pay dividends means that the proportion spent on these is lower than it would otherwise be and certainly lower than it should be; especially after years of chronic under-funding. Problems, meanwhile, are never the operator's fault, but the result of the weather or the network. Complaints result in a mandated payment according to the regulator, but there is no concept of using these as a source to improve service.

At the same time road congestion has increased with ever more cars on the roads. Inter-city travel times have probably doubled in the past 10 years while inner city travel is officially now slower than the days of the horse drawn carriage, with average speeds continuing to decline. This is not helped by reductions of speed limits in urban areas from 30 to 20 miles per hour and the introduction of "sleeping policemen." These will destroy the sump or gear box and crush the vertebrae of the driver and passengers in any car exceeding this. Ostensibly this is to improve road safety, but is really another hidden tax intended to swell the municipal coffers through fines for the more intrepid prepared to risk their health and their vehicle's by going faster. This is self-evident since cars are better designed, safer and can stop quicker than ever before. On top of this there are congestion charges, tolls and exorbitant parking costs, all of which would make cars an expensive luxury if public transport offered a viable alternative. It is hardly any wonder that road rage is increasing and more and more people try to make up lost time on the motorways. Unfortunately this often simply increases the risk of accidents and adds additional hours to the travelling time.

Now these are all very different problems but they all have one thing in common: they are potentially extremely costly to fix and will put a strain on the national coffers. Those cited are clearly British problems, and I am able to write about them more easily because I live in Britain and so am more aware of them. But I don't for a moment think they are unique to Britain. They simply may be more visible because of its size, the greater density of its population, and its more open democracy. The riots in Greece and France in 2008 suggest that other countries in Europe are facing similar problems. They may not be exactly the same and they may vary in scale or nature, but the underlying currents are there; not least in the sublimation of national identity in the attempt to strengthen the European Union.

Of course Britain and the US probably have closer cultural and political links than any other two nations on earth and the similarities here are more evident. The US does not have the socialistic fusion that Britain has, but that has created its own political stress. The rampant capitalism, with the greed that has underpinned it and that is now more obvious for all to see, has created a greater divide between the haves and the have-nots. The underclass and socially excluded are there too, if not in the same guise. On top of that there is the rural versus urban divide which creates a further dichotomy and radicalism that doesn't exist in Britain. This led to the "home-grown" terrorism highlighted by Timothy McVey and the Oklahoma bombing and the US needs to take care that this does not recur or proliferate.

Clearly then the water temperature has been rising for all of us. Perhaps the global recession is a blessing in that it has created an awareness of this fact and these issues that didn't exist before. There is no doubt that it is going to make things more difficult than they would otherwise have been. There is, however, no way to avoid them and we need to start looking at new ways to do things now. We also need to recognise and accept the interconnection between all these issues and acknowledge that trying to solve one on its own without looking at the totality is like squeezing a balloon. We need to remove the dirt from the picture of the world and look at it anew.

PART 3
Solutions

The Basis for a Solution

"The problem is not that there are problems.
The problem is expecting otherwise and thinking
that having a problem is a problem."

THEODORE RUBIN

I have used the frog analogy as a theme in this book because when I first started writing it seemed that so many of the issues that I was concerned about were simply being ignored. Lately, however, it seems that many of them are coming to the surface and, happily, more consideration seems to be being given to a wider range of possible solutions. As a result I began to wonder if the metaphor was no longer appropriate. I have persisted with it because I believe it remains equally valid and because I feel there is still a need to draw attention to the possibility that we may in many cases be overlooking the root cause.

It may perhaps be easier to understand both my concerns and my suggested solutions if I take a little time-out to explain where my ideas first started.

In the early nineteen nineties we were living in Ontario, Canada, having emigrated from South Africa. Inevitably we found things different, and as newcomers were particularly sensitive to things that we might otherwise have taken for granted. One of those things we were very aware of was that as we endeavoured to start afresh, establish ourselves and build up a new personal infrastructure, we were some way behind those who had been there longer and really disadvantaged against those who had been born or raised there. This was naturally compounded by the fact that the unfavourable exchange rate had literally halved our net worth and we were thus inevitably more conscious of the need to save and build up. Consequently our income was vital. I was therefore particularly struck by the tax system and the way that tax was levied at both a national and a provincial level. While both were reasonable on their own, their combined effect was quite painful. As things changed over time, I became more aware of this and, as each made changes, used to ask myself whether they understood that there was really still only one taxpayer.

As I became more involved in the community and local chamber of commerce, I also realised how the divide complicated the socio-economic and political decision making. The net effect is to make everything more complicated and ultimately more costly. All this made me very aware of the amount I paid in taxes and how government misspent (wasted) that money. This feeling was reinforced when we moved to Britain. Thus I strongly believe that government owes it to its citizens to use the money it takes from them wisely. In the same way that directors owe it to their shareholders to optimise their resources to maximise profits, governments and charities have a duty to use donations wisely and efficiently, governments have a moral obligation to their people to use their resources efficiently.

Clearly this leaves me firmly in the Conservative camp with a fundamental philosophy that the less government involvement there is in the economy the better. I ultimately want to look after my own destiny and want as little government interference in my affairs as possible. Yet it isn't as clear-cut as that.

In the late nineties I was working as a consultant for Oracle when we were asked by the development team to review the beta site for Boo.com, a new clothing dot.com fashion site that was about to be launched. As I did so, I was forcibly struck by the realisation that the business model was unsound. This start-up company was spending a fortune on launching a business on the basis of creating a whole new market of online shoppers. This was all very well and good, but they were also failing to recognise that there is still only "one customer". I became very conscious that business leaders seemed to have no understanding of basic economics and the fact that, as a consumer, I only had a limited amount available to spend.

Of course this insight was totally vindicated when Boo became one of the early casualties of the dot.com bust just a few weeks later. Unfortunately, the bubble bursting was blamed on over-enthusiasm in new technology overriding common sense. Very few seemed to recognise the endemic lack of economic understanding and the greed that persisted despite the lesson. "Rip-off Britain" remained alive and well, and based on the chickens coming home to roost in the US recently, it was very much the same on that side of the Atlantic. Very few seemed to recognise that unlimited credit can only grow an economy to a certain point before the whole edifice will come tumbling down like a pack of cards. Although now, just like Germans who claimed they had no idea what Hitler was up to, everyone is donning their hair-suits and claiming they did see it coming, only not just yet.

Consequently, I am equally firmly convinced that, unless there are proper checks and balances, the market is an ass and that the capitalist philosophy is fundamentally unsound. This makes me anything but a typical conservative.

However, I may be being too quick to jump to conclusions here, for the problem may not be with the free market itself, but rather the way it has been deregulated. In his book "Democratic Capitalism: The Way to a World of Peace and Plenty"[17], Ray

---

[17] Democratic Capitalism: The Way to a World of Peace and Plenty P 467 Ray Carey ©2004 Author House

Carey claims, *"Conservatives and market fundamentalists have stolen the good phrase free markets, for they pretend to free the world's capital market, while they, at the same time, contradict economic freedom through their reliance on federal insurance, subsidies and bailouts."* (P 467) Carey makes a strong case that "ultra-capitalism", through powerful lobbying by Wall Street, has led to the US government making mistakes and creating bad policies that resulted in the deregulation and abrogation of market disciplines, thus wasting the opportunity created by the collapse of communism and destabilising the international monetary system by making speculators more powerful than central bankers and creating greater inequality of wealth than ever before.

So where does that leave me? Clearly not a socialist and certainly not a conservative, but probably not a social democrat either. So what else is there? An anarchist? I don't think so but I leave it to the reader to decide! It all just goes to show how our attempts to categorise things serves to narrow our thinking and preclude other alternatives.

However, let's forget about categorising things for a moment, and go back to the point that I was making. In each case there was a common thread: that there is only one of me. And that is the essence of it. No matter what the government or the business is trying to get from me, their potential is limited by that fact. As a consumer or a tax payer the revenue that I create for them is determined by my finite resources. They might be able to stimulate me to do more (unlikely in the government's case!) but sooner or later a limit is reached. If pushed beyond that point the consequences are bad for both parties. And of course that is the lesson the collapsed financial markets are now driving home to everyone who forgot. This is vital to understand, because the solution to these problems also ultimately rests with us as the individual consumers and taxpayers. The easy credit has to be paid for and is now impinging our ability to pay for the solution. Consequently the solution involves everyone and thus needs the "buy-in" of the man in the street if it has to have any chance of succeeding.

That is why I began the book by describing the failure of democracy. Somehow we have to find a way to build new structures that will reinforce the fundamentals of true democracy, where the good of the larger community takes precedence over the individual but without belittling or superseding the individual's rights. That requires a new balance, because it is the too rigid enforcement of individual rights that has led us into this predicament.

It is this, as much as the easy credit and the easy living, that has gone a long way towards bankrupting us morally. It is perhaps a bit of cliché to talk about the me generation, and the case against is rightly and strongly made by examples of people whose actions are anything but selfish. Yet selfishness takes many forms and the consequences speak for themselves. These are perhaps summed this up best in this recent chain email attributed to George Carlin, the American comedian.

The paradox of our time in history is that we have taller buildings but shorter tempers; wider freeways, but narrower viewpoints. We spend more, but have less; we buy more, but enjoy less. We have bigger houses and smaller families; more conveniences but less time. We have more degrees but less sense; more knowledge, but less judgment; more experts, yet more problems; more medicine, but less wellness.

We drink too much, smoke too much, spend too recklessly, laugh too little, drive too fast, get too angry, stay up too late, get up too tired, read too little, watch TV too much, and pray too seldom.

We have multiplied our possessions, but reduced our values. We talk too much, love too seldom, and hate too often.

We've learned how to make a living, but not a life. We've added years to life not life to years. We've been all the way to

---

the moon and back, but have trouble crossing the street to meet a new neighbour. We conquered outer space but not inner space. We've done larger things, but not better things.

We've cleaned up the air, but polluted the soul. We've conquered the atom, but not our prejudice. We write more, but learn less. We plan more, but accomplish less. We've learned to rush, but not to wait. We build more computers to hold more information, to produce more copies than ever, but we communicate less and less.

These are the times of fast foods and slow digestion; big men and small character; steep profits and shallow relationships. These are the days of two incomes but more divorce; fancier houses, but broken homes. These are days of quick trips, disposable diapers, throwaway morality, one night stands, overweight bodies, and pills that do everything from cheer, to quiet, to kill. It is a time when there is much in the showroom window and nothing in the stockroom.

George Carlin, American Comedian

This is an interesting piece from someone who regularly lampooned religion, for it actually has a very strong moral and ethical message. For me the essence of what he is saying is that we have become too self-absorbed. Thus it is not necessarily selfishness per se that has corrupted things, but the tendency to judge things solely by the way in which they affect us. This is what creates intolerance for the other person's situation, viewpoint or circumstances.

Unfortunately this is just as true of organised religion as any other sector of society. Churches that preach love and tolerance towards our fellow man are prime examples of intolerance. You only have to look at the divisive issues of women priests, homosexuality and inter-faith conflict to see that the fundamental teachings have been subsumed. This has done irreparable damage. I grant you there has always been hypocrisy, but mass communication publicises it more, and so more people than ever before move away from the bastions that have helped make civilisation possible.

The master Christian taught that the second great commandment was like the first, and was, "Thou shalt love thy neighbour as thyself". That to me means on the same level - not as a poor second. Yet this is forgotten by Christians and Muslims (for whom he was also their greatest prophet after Mohammad) alike. It is hardly surprising that church adherence is declining and children are increasingly ignorant about these great lessons of human interaction.

Consequently everything boils down to a question of personal rights and everyone forgets that rights have to be balanced by obligations and that others have the same rights.

The problems identified in this book and Carlin's list all stem from too much self-importance and too little self-worth. The great paradox of life is that we derive most satisfaction from our actions that bring other people pleasure. The joy of an experience shared is nearly always greater than one experienced on one's own and we ultimately judge our own worth on our ability to please others and so make a difference. Thus the primary theme of this book – as the title suggests – is to find solutions that help people to attain a greater sense of their self-worth. I believe this is the only way that we will be able to rescue ourselves from the hot water before it is too late.

Hopefully there will be a few other like-minded people after you have completed the book, and we can help launch a new wave of thinking and acting. *"Small people talk about people. Average people talk about events. Great people talk about ideas."* I don't know who the author of that quote is but let us prove that we are great people and develop some great ideas together.

The Basis for a Solution

CHAPTER NINE

Business Worth

"Happiness lies not in the mere possession of money; it lies in the joy of achievement, in the thrill of creative effort. The joy and moral stimulation of work no longer must be forgotten in the mad chase of evanescent profits. These dark days will be worth all they cost us if they teach us that our true destiny is not to be ministered unto but to minister to ourselves and to our fellow men."

FRANKLIN D ROOSEVELT: FIRST INAUGURAL SPEECH

Roosevelt's words contain an important lesson that I think we have all forgotten. Business is ultimately the provision of products or services to people by people. Thus at the end of the day it is all very much about people. Consequently if we take the joy and moral stimulation away we destroy people's self worth and it all becomes a meaningless grind.

This is what has been happening. Numerous surveys show that employee engagement is low and getting lower. The Towers Perrin 2007 Global Workforce Study showed that, globally, 79% of the workforce is disengaged. Put that the other way and it tells you that only 21% of the workforce is engaged. How on earth do you expect to provide a competitive offering and retain customer loyalty if only one fifth of your people are committed to doing so?

Even more frightening 38% are 'actively disengaged'. This means that, if people are not actively sabotaging the business, they are not that far removed from doing so. Do you remember the once popular saying, "It is difficult to drain the swamp when you are up to your arse in alligators"? Well, trying to run a business in these circumstances must come pretty close!

Now, while you might look to find some comfort in the fact that these are global figures and therefore an average, do not be fooled into thinking that they do not apply where you are. The engagement figure in Britain is below average, but the figures generally do not make encouraging reading. As the following table[18] shows, it is clearly a case of "Houston, we have a problem". Across the world it would appear that we are not using people very effectually, and that has to have an enormous economic (and commercial) cost to the businesses themselves.

Country	Engaged %	Disengaged %	Ratio
Canada	23	7	3.29
China	16	6	2.67
France	12	12	1.00
Germany	17	8	8.50
India	36	3	12.00
Italy	11	13	-1.18
Japan	3	16	-5.34
Russia	18	7	2.57
S. Korea	8	7	1.14
UK	14	11	1.27
USA	29	6	4.83
Average	**17**	**8.7**	**1.95**

This table perhaps shows the dangers of extrapolating figures across whole populations on a statistical basis from sample testing - something that we are very prone to do, and which

---

[18] Data taken from the Towers Perrin Global Workforce Study 2007-2008

all too often drives government policy. The unexpectedly high engagement figures in India, China and Russia may reflect a tendency to be grateful for having work at all, although even here the figures are hardly encouraging. In many ways, however, these findings are ironic, because corporate 'HR' policies are probably more enlightened than at any time in history. Earnings packages are more flexible than ever before and there is increasing recognition of the need for "work-life balance". So what is undermining all these efforts?

The reasons will naturally vary from organisation to organisation and country to country and provide a long list. I submit, however, that such a list could be simply summed up in the fact that their work environment contributes little or nothing to a person's sense of self-worth. Such a feeling may be engendered by any one or more of:

- Being regarded as a 'resource' rather than a person. (Whoever coined the phrase 'Human Resources' in preference to 'Personnel' has a lot to explain, as does the rest of the profession for accepting it.)

- Constant change, which is often imposed rather than facilitated and thus leaves people uninvolved and thus detached.

- The pressures on performance and improvement, most of which have been driven from above with little understanding of the issues the people face on a daily basis.

- Witnessing themselves or their colleagues being treated as expendable through redundancy and reduction programmes undertaken in the pursuit of greater profits.

In his latest book, "The Future of Management" Gary Hamel identifies the need, *"to co-ordinate the efforts of thousands of individuals without creating a burdensome hierarchy of overseers; to build companies that liberate human imagination while keeping a tight rein on costs; and to invent organisations where discipline and freedom are not mutually exclusive."* He argues that, *"For the first time since the dawning of the industrial age the only way to build a company that is fit for the future is to build one that's fit for human beings as well. This is your opportunity – to build a management system that truly honours and cherishes human initiative, creativity and passion, essential ingredients for success in the new millennium."*[19]

I believe there is a very simple solution to this. As outlined in "Lean Organisations Need FAT People" it is quite straightforward to start valuing people as assets rather than just referring to them as such. In fact I am building a business to help organisations properly and consistently value their people, so I do not want to dwell on this too much. However, it behoves me to explain a little about the proposition, which offers:

1. The capability to value people individually and collectively. This creates a basis for making the so-called 'intangible' assets tangible, and brings the management of people into line with the management of other assets.

2. The option to make people co-owners of the business, at no direct cost to them or the business.

3. The option to create a 'labour dividend'. Basically this is a form of profit sharing tied to a person's individual value. It is more equitable than any other such scheme, because it is objective. The person's value is empirically determined by a transparent process that cannot be varied or manipulated. Thus it

---

[19] "The Future of Management" Gary Hamel with Bill Breen, Harvard Business School Press © 2007

does not have the traditional weaknesses of other performance related remuneration schemes.

The three offerings are independent although, obviously, they hinge on the concept of valuing people, which is intrinsic to all three.[20]

The key points to note with this approach are:

- It self-evidently goes a long way towards addressing the fundamental causes of employee disengagement. It encourages organisation and individual alike to optimise their value and in the process inculcates recognition of worth.

- It provides a basis for overcoming the short-term thinking that has so dominated the commercial world in recent decades and which has finally been exposed by the current economic crisis.

This approach provides the essential first step to creating the new management model that Professor Hamel is calling for. It compels worker and manager alike to collaborate to optimise the individual, and so reverses the traditional conflict between the two.

In their book, "Growing your Own Heroes"[21] John Oliver and Clive Memmott claim that the *"key driver to successful implementation is not the sophistication and technical excellence of your structures, but the spirit and intent behind them."* In other words, the purpose. They identify that this requires:

- A genuine approach,

- A real opportunity for involvement,

---

[20] Readers who are interested in learning more about these concepts are recommended to go to my website at *www.zealise.com*

[21] "Growing Your Own Heroes: The Common Sense Way to Improve Business Performance" John J Oliver and Clive Memmott Oaktree Press © 2006

- Real opportunities to "make a difference",

- The contribution to be valued.

I would paraphrase that as creating a feeling of worth, but however you express it, valuing and treating people as assets meets these requirements in spades. In one of their case studies they emphasise the need to ensure there is a structure behind the philosophy, for, *"Without being embedded into routine, the sceptics and cynics prevail."* This approach fuses philosophy and structure perfectly.

ADDRESSING SHORT-TERM THINKING

The recent collapse of the financial markets has, hopefully, exposed for once and for all, the fallacy of managing for 'shareholder value'. This closed the divide between management and shareholder thinking. It placed business executives firmly in the same camp as the shareholders and has mitigated their responsibility to balance the short-term and the long-term.

For many of the large public companies the measure of shareholder value is the share price. Consequently too much emphasis has been placed on maintaining and growing the share price, which in turn has been seen a way of enhancing credibility and thereby helping grow business. This has led to constant pressure to deliver quarter on quarter growth, and all manner of ingenious schemes to ensure this. For the financial institutions this has been the development of new and increasingly risky products and services, specifically including the so-called sub-prime lending in the US. Here in the UK the banks have bolstered their figures by issuing loans on 100% of the value of properties, at multiples of salaries. All premised on the belief that the market would continue rising, this exposed borrowers to totally unacceptable risk. Yet, like an alcoholic in a free bar, 'the market' allowed it to happen and blindly followed with never a thought to the consequences.

This short-term thinking also affected the institutional investors. In order to maintain their competitive edge and attract more funds they had to resort to doing everything they could to increase their returns. This led to share churning on an unprecedented scale and fuelled an over-inflated stock exchange and reinforced executives' efforts to do all they could to bolster share prices. All this created a dangerous vicious cycle. As I said before, it became a form of pyramid selling on its own, even before the latest scandal of real pyramid selling that occurred within one of the largest hedge funds.

If those forces were not bad enough on their own, they were exacerbated by the share plans and share option schemes which formed a key part of executives' pay. Justified by the ingenious (and ingenuous) argument that this "encourages managers to think more like owners" this finally destroyed any major difference between executive and shareholder thinking. Management's primary role to look after businesses' long-term interests was subverted. A higher share price meant more for those who were supposed to keep the checks and balances and removed the final restraints to greed.

Thus everything became one massive trough. The major focus became one of keeping the trends going and suppressing bad news. Babe Ruth used to say; "Every strikeout brings me closer to the next home run." This was the complete opposite, with every new scheme, dubious deal or bad news cover-up making the collapse of the whole edifice ever more likely. Indeed, an inside account of the collapse of Lehman Brothers had the headline, "Caught in the death spiral."[22] That of course is what a vicious circle inevitably becomes, no matter which direction it is initially moving.

This report actually gives a fascinating insight into the culture prevailing at the time of Lehman's collapse by Andrew

---

[22] Sunday Times News Review 14 December 2008

Gowers, a former Financial Times Editor who worked there. It is worth quoting in part, for it states, *"The Lehman culture had become dangerously complacent and insulated from the outside world. While Fuld (the CEO) talked to clients with legendary assiduity, neither he nor Gregory (his number two) spent much time talking (still less listening) to investors. Even within the firm, Fuld's visits to the trading floor were rare events. So he was shut off from independent sources of information, from challenging questions and from up-to-date views from the front line of Lehman's daily battle in the market. He was fed instead with the carefully filtered facts that his inner circle thought he wanted to hear. Furthermore the top team was not united."*

Making people assets and co-owners of the business is a very effective way of countering this trend. This might seem like a contradiction, since you could say that it will now put *everyone* in the same camp. However, the lower ranks in an organisation tend to remain working there for longer and thus have more of a vested interest in the longer-term. So they are more likely to consider the longer-term perspective, particularly if they now have the commitment and pride of ownership that means they see the organisation as their own business.

There is, of course, no guarantee that this will prevent an Enron type culture from developing. However, if nothing else, this will reduce the risk of rogue elements (including executives) hijacking the culture and values, simply because the weight of numbers will make it less likely. The odds of this could also be strengthened by tying in ownership with pension provision. This is something that could be part of the people asset/ownership scheme and if introduced would play a major role in counterbalancing the short term focus that has soured business and ruined so many lives for so long.

There is undoubtedly a risk in so closely aligning people's everyday work with their retirement savings. But it is questionable whether it is any more risky than leaving them to be invested by rash fund investors or in apparently safe corporations that turn out not to be as safe as everyone thinks. Life is a series of risks, and making people take greater responsibility for their own circumstances, current and future, will hopefully encourage greater accountability and, with it, greater wisdom. It will certainly reduce the scale of misfortune witnessed in this most recent economic maelstrom.

OTHER UNRECOGNISED SHORT-TERM THINKING

I stated earlier that valuing people as assets both addresses the root causes of employee engagement and insidious short-term thinking. There is one particular area where it does both simultaneously: in situations where redundancy or mass layoffs are a key plank in management efforts to address business problems.

Mass layoffs or redundancy has been an option for owners and business managers since the start of the industrial revolution, and a common phenomenon during the last 30 years or more. A new economic downturn sees it once again becoming widespread, and it is clearly one of management's primary counter-recessionary tools. The question is, "Why?"

It would be foolish to deny there may be times when layoffs are unavoidable, but their ultimate effectiveness and validity is worth questioning. There are actually five reasons why it needs to be more carefully considered before it is invoked.

1. The Need to Rethink Selection Criteria

Personal experience, as both implementer and victim, suggests the decision and selection processes are hasty and ill-conceived. When working in a large retail bank I witnessed the entire private banking function being discarded, just as break-even was reached after 3 years of investment. The staff had been hand-selected as the best in the company, but when challenged, my manager simply told me that, "we don't have time to be more selective!"

2. Questionable Commercial Logic

The commercial perspective is equally dubious. The premise is to incur extraordinary costs now to reduce future costs. Yet no break-even analysis is ever done to correlate cost savings to the expected duration of the difficulties. It also seems counter-intuitive to do this when business is declining and profits need boosting, rather than reducing. Furthermore, it makes no economic or commercial sense to effectively pay people not to do anything, as redundancy pay does. This is compounded by the fact decisions are usually made without any regard to the investment already made in the people being retrenched.

3. Overlooking the Long-term Implications

Decisions to lay people off also ignore the possibly vital contribution to any turnaround or future efforts that they might make. In fact research indicates that businesses that layoff people in a recession take longer to 'snap back' and remain less competitive when the economy recovers.

4. Its impact on Morale and Motivation

The motivation and morale aspects are considered but not always properly assessed. No businesses operating in an ever more competitive global environment can afford to compound the problem of poor employee engagement. Mass layoffs will do this and also damage the recruiter's 'employer brand'. With the looming 'war for talent' a business cannot afford to lose its recruiting edge. This creates a double whammy that has further long-term implications.

5. The Wider Economic Impact

Laying people off also has a wider economic impact, exacerbating the downturn, making it deeper and more long-lasting than it would otherwise be. It is the direct opposite to what Henry Ford proved in 1914, when he doubled his workers' hourly rate and restricted their standard shifts to 8 hours.

So clearly redundancy is counter-productive, for the organisations themselves and their long-term prospects, and for the wider community. It is indicative of short-term thinking and should only be used in dire circumstances, when it is the only possible way to survive in the short-term and may mean operating on a different basis/scale in the longer term. That it is so commonplace is thus cause for concern. Clearly alternative solutions need to be found.

Valuing and treating people as assets offers such an alternative and, amongst its other benefits, will counteract the short-term thinking to:

- Change the mindset that continues to regard people solely as a cost, compel greater consideration of the value of what is proposed to be discarded, and encourage use of existing capabilities to meet the challenges rather than dissipating them.

- Break the unthinking habit of using redundancy as a remedy for bad times, with no thought as to the wider economic costs.

- Enable greater management focus on strategic issues.

Of course this will not remove the fundamental problems that cause layoffs. It does, however, reduce the likelihood, frequency and scale of redundancy as a remedy for business problems. This compels better selection and people management after they are recruited, and creates more long-term thinking within the business. It aligns better with management's primary responsibility to safeguard the organisation's assets, and enables managers and shareholders alike to better assess the value of the human assets they propose to jettison. This makes management more accountable for these decisions and compels alternative solutions to be sought. It also makes them considerably easier to implement.[23] It also provides a platform for ensuring the organisation is better placed to snap back when the economy recovers.

That is not all it will do either, but to understand its further merits we need to look at the wider implications of looking at people as assets.

ASSETS VERSUS COSTS

Let's take a moment to look at the basics and start by distinguishing between assets and costs.

An asset is defined as a commodity acquired for ongoing use in the business. It is consumed over time in the course of operations:

- Directly to manufacture or deliver a product or service intended to generate income; or

- Indirectly to further other operations that manufacture or deliver products or services, or support the administration of the general business of manufacturing or supplying products or services.

A cost is a one-time expense legitimately incurred:

- Directly in the production of a product or service intended to be sold; or

- Indirectly in the maintenance of an asset or in support of the production or delivery of a product or service or the administration of the general business of manufacturing and supplying products or services.

So the distinction is a very fine one that can be broadly boiled down to the fact an expense has a one time use, whereas an

---

[23] Readers who are interested in learning more about the alternatives to redundancy and why valuing people as assets will make them easier to implement, should go to my website *www.alternativestoredundancy.com*

asset has an ongoing usefulness. The major differentiation comes in the accounting treatment, because a cost is expensed in its entirety the moment it is either purchased or consumed. An asset on the other hand has its cost used up gradually over what is regarded as its "expected useful life" and this cost is charged through the accounts as depreciation.

Historically, however, people – despite their ongoing contribution to the business – have been regarded, and treated, as a cost. They are employed on an open-ended hire contract and their monthly 'hire' is expensed until such time as either party terminates the contract.

This has its origins in the fact that labour was often itinerant; few skills were required; and so people could be easily replaced and seamlessly take over one from another.

As roles have become more knowledge based and workers have become more skilled this has become increasingly inappropriate. Losing a worker has significant implications for a business and its capabilities. Managers and executives have thus become increasingly prone to regarding their people as assets and even referring to them as such. They are increasingly being recognised as being what gives a business its competitive edge. As a result "Human Capital Management" (HCM) and reporting has become a much debated subject. Despite this people continue to be regarded as costs and their treatment, accounting or otherwise, reflects this attitude.

INAPPROPRIATENESS OF ACCOUNTING FOR PEOPLE AS COSTS

In light of all this it hardly seems appropriate to continue to account for people as costs. They clearly make an ongoing contribution to the business and are more than mere costs. But, as we have just seen, although there is an intellectual acceptance of the idea of people as assets, this has not yet translated into any definitive action. And, the readiness to make people redundant that I described earlier clearly shows that, despite this intellectual acceptance, behaviour is very far removed.

In fact companies are only able to make people redundant because they think of them as costs. Few companies dispense with a significant part of their asset base when a recession strikes, because it doesn't make sense to erode productive capabilities. Yet there is no compunction to do this with people, which shows just how far attitudes need to change.

It seems inhumane to treat people so cavalierly; hiring in good times and firing in the bad. Do you realise that it actually could be interpreted that we treat inanimate objects more kindly? Joking aside, though, does it not seem unkind at best and uncivilised at worst that we should treat people that way? It may be relatively easy to reduce production or mothball a plant during quiet times, but the point is you still have them when the good times return. Thus you have the capability to return to full production relatively easily when they do. If people are the assets we claim them to be we should follow the same practice with them.

It is interesting that Europe, while not quite as liberal as this, tends to treat people more like assets. Indeed the argument about the freedom to hire and fire is perhaps one of the major causes of Britain's reluctance to commit totally to Europe and enter the Eurozone. It is an area where Britain and the US have more in common; but one has to ask whether this is perhaps not a major reason for the fact that those two countries are being hardest hit by the economic downturn? In their efforts to keep employment levels high, have they perhaps built greater inefficiencies into their economies and kept them hidden by allowing the economy to grow unrealistically? This would imply more sinister policies than poor regulation in allowing borrowing to reach the levels they did. Not a nice thought!

WHY ACCOUNT FOR PEOPLE AS ASSETS

We have already seen that treating people as costs and laying them off during a recession is actually counter-productive. Accounting for them as assets will help avert that waste, and so is one obvious reason. However there is another, for treating people as a cost results in businesses understating their true economic costs.

Let's take a topical example of a cyclical industry like the motor trade. Currently these companies are on reduced shifts or operating plant shutdowns, in order to reduce production and try to avoid layoffs. Ignoring the question of whether these companies have historically over-produced, their immediate challenge is that they have far too great a stockpile of completed cars for sale and a capability to produce many, many more. Unfortunately, the economic climate means they are unable to sell the cars they have already made let alone sell any additional ones they could make now. This is what I meant earlier when I said that the commercial world was now getting back into equilibrium with the economic world.

The fact is that economically these idle times are actually part of the cost of production but have never been factored in. The benefits of scale of mass production impel the company to produce as many cars as it can in order to keep the unit costs down. After all, the lower the cost the lower the selling price need be and hence the greater the perceived value and the more cars they are likely to sell. Production targets are then set based on complex models integrating all the elements of plant capability, unit costs, selling price and projected sales. This is great while the good times roll and the company *is* able to keep its unit costs down *and* sell the cars it produces. However, plants are tooled up and staffed for what ultimately turns out to be a greater production than the market can bear. That is when the chickens come home to roost.

This is because unit costs increase dramatically as soon as production slows and rocket when no cars are being produced and costs are still being incurred. Thus the average unit cost is higher than was initially calculated and the selling price is inadequate to generate profit. So we get a boom and bust at a micro-level within the industry. The company does its best to keep costs to a minimum in order to reduce this effect and maintain its commercial position, but they are non-productive costs and cannot be easily recovered.

The unit cost would be considerably higher if the total costs were averaged over a complete economic cycle, and consequently the selling price would likely also be considerably higher. Hence the costs are understated and the profits false. The ultimate effect here is that the wider economy is effectively subsidising the industry. The buyer would unquestionably have to pay a higher price if the true costs were calculated. The recession gives the industry time to realign with the economy. On a wider scale that is effectively bringing the commerce into line with the economics.

However, the problem is that as part of the process these companies usually end up laying off workers. This is part of the effort to keep those non-productive costs down. Thus they continue to work on a reduced workforce and skeleton capacity until such time as the market rebounds and they are able to start selling more cars and building up production once again to reduce the unit costs. At this stage they will start rehiring. As we have already established this is unproductive to the company over the long-term, this means that the total cost to the economy is actually greater than it need have been. This is on top of the fact that by offloading people during the bad times the industry is effectively relying on the wider economy to pick up those costs it would have incurred if it used people on a more consistent and humane basis. To avoid this we have to find a more accurate way of accounting for these total costs and accounting for people as assets is part of that process.

HOW TO 'MOTHBALL' PEOPLE ASSETS

Let's now assume that these people are assets. This changes the whole approach to the way they are managed. They will now be regarded in the same light as other assets and will only be dispensed with in exceptional circumstances. Instead, like most other assets, they have to be 'mothballed'. This means that those costs cannot be eliminated, but have to be covered in another way. This clearly necessitates some sort of salary cut but with a retainer paid for the duration. While this sounds preposterous it is simply a means to try to align the commercial costs with the economic ones and to that extent is simply a method of keeping the cost in the company rather than the community. So the ultimate objective is simply to try to spread the total costs for the entire cycle. This will eliminate the industry boom and bust cycle or, at worst, flatten the curve and so reduce the severity of the difference between the highs and the lows.

This can be done by paying an additional proportion of a person's earnings into a 'payroll equalisation fund'. This is effectively an accounting reserve that acts as a corporate 'savings fund'. It allows money to be set aside in the good times so salaries can be paid and expensed during times of low production, rather than laying people off. This enables a company to:

- Offer a more equitable company-wide salary cut rather than having an unfortunate proportion lose their jobs completely.

- Pay people an additional amount to offset the impact of the salary cut.

- Retain all its assets for the time when production can increase once more.

It also means the company retains the intelligent capability to undertake other activities or develop new ideas or business opportunities to help the business in the longer term. Let me explain with a simple hypothetical example.

XYZ has 1,000 people registered as assets at the start of the recession, but due to the recession only has enough work for 800. Historically this might have meant laying off the 'surplus' 200. Instead it can now:

- Introduce a company wide salary cut of 20%.[24]

- Utilise a 'payroll equalisation reserve' to offset that salary cut.[25]

- Work with all 1000 people to develop and implement new ideas to offset the lost business, and develop the business and place it in a better position to compete effectively.

If you are not convinced that there is a case for this, let me show you some further grounds.

THE REALITY OF GOVERNMENT RECESSIONARY SPENDING

We have seen that not only does redundancy not often make commercial sense, but it also exacerbates and extends the effects of an economic downturn. It is therefore pertinent to look more closely at the economic effects.

Roosevelt's words at the beginning of the chapter seem particularly appropriate now, as a new US president steps into office in the worst economic climate since those "dark days" of the Great Depression. With the "evanescence" of the

---

[24] Once again I would urge readers who would like to know more about how treating people as assets will facilitate this to go to my website *www.alternativestoredundancy.com*

[25] I suppose it would be possible to use this to offset only a proportion of the salary cut but this would mean we only achieve part of the desired effect of accounting for the true economic costs of this idle time.

banking industry's profits reaching such extremes that they required a trillion dollar bailout, the situation is certainly bleak. There is still the fifteen billion dollar bailout requested for the US Motor industry but already the US government has had to borrow the equivalent of more than $3,000 for every man, woman and child. This is no small legacy to leave future generations to pay. On top of that, however, one needs to remember that:

- Conventional wisdom has it that the best (only?) way out of a recession is to spend. Unfortunately, even in a capitalist economy like the US, it would appear that the onus is on government to do this spending.

- There are still the previously uncharged costs of climate change to be paid for.

Consequently, this is going to be more difficult for governments to do than ever before. This is because the proportion of GDP that government takes is already at historically high levels. Remember it is forecast to be 38.3% for the UK for 2009, and that was before the British government's bailout of British banks. As governments do not have their own revenue base and ultimately have to get their money from the people – yep, you and me! – this means the water is getting uncomfortably hot for us human frogs. Remember, there is only one of each of us, so there has to be a limit as to how much government can squeeze from us. And even when it borrows it has to pay it back along with the interest, so ultimately we all have to pay all these costs. All of which underscores a need to reassess the whole dynamic of the profit equation and how we run business.

These corporate bailouts in the US, UK, Europe and Japan are perhaps the most glaring example in history of the disparity between economics and commerce. As we saw in Chapter 5 profit is totally a commercial concept that does not exist in economics. Consequently it is no wonder that economies are subject to cycles of economic boom and bust as the two shift towards some level of equilibrium. If you accept that premise you will understand why, after the longest period of sustained growth in history, the economy has swung so suddenly and viciously into recession. It is also why you will appreciate the need to do more to bring commerce and economics into greater alignment.

There may not be a way to eliminate commercial profit completely, but doing whatever we can to close some of the gap, will mitigate the degree of swing in these economic cycles.

ANOTHER LOOK AT FALSE PROFITS

Few businesses, if any, have consistent profits. They tend to move up and down as economic and trading conditions vary over time. Thus theoretically a company's commercial profit can only be measured over its entire existence. For example a company that makes a million profit one year and a half a million loss the next year only averages a quarter of a million profit over the two years. As it only pays corporation tax in the year it makes a profit it is thus an inconsistent contributor to the national exchequer. Thus to properly assess its contribution to the treasury one would need to take an average over an extended period. The longer the period the more likely you will be to get a true sense of the company's profitability.

As we have just seen, the motor industry is particularly volatile and subject to extreme swings between profits and losses. Thus one would really need to assess its contribution to the treasury over an extended period to see to what extent any kind of bailout is justified. In any event, a bailout of say $5 billion to General Motors would have the effect of recapitalising the company and so suggests any one or more of the following:

- Accumulated profits have been insufficient and therefore the business has not been as profitable as has been reported;

- Too much has been paid out in dividends in earlier years;

- Too much buying back of their own shares;

- The directors have mismanaged the business;

- The business is no longer viable;

- (As with climate change) costs have historically been understated and now need to be accounted for.

Without knowing the answers to any of these points it is actually impossible to determine whether a bailout is appropriate. Certainly the fact that General Motors has spent billions buying back its own shares, as part of a trend that saw US companies buy back $1.7 *trillion* worth of their own shares between 2003 and 2007, would suggest that it is not. The bankrupt financial services companies bailed out by the US government had themselves spent $43 billion in that manner.[26] Whatever the outcome, the situation tends to confirm my assertion that the costs have not been correctly calculated – and therefore, by definition, neither have profits.

Although by no means an expert on the motor industry, I think I can safely say that most people understand that car manufacturers actually sell cars at less than their true (commercial) cost. Anyone who has bought parts knows that the sum of the cost of parts is considerably greater than the cost of the whole. It is accepted wisdom that car manufacturers make the bulk of their profits from their finance arms which have encouraged people to borrow. Thus, regardless of whether you accept the earlier explanation of the motor industry as

---

[26] Facts taken from the article "Corporate Apocalypse" published in Management Today: January 2009

prima facie evidence of poor economic accounting, it is clear that their business model is open to challenge.

As an industry they have all been flogging cars at a far greater rate than they could possibly have done if we had to pay the true cost and if we had not had access to the easy loans they provided. They would have us believe that this 'subsidy' has been recovered by the part sales and dealership servicing. But the proliferation of other independent parts manufacturers must have seriously compromised that ability. Consequently the question has to be asked, whether these bailouts are not simply the result of these poor business practices? Perhaps it is tantamount to government now being asked to pick up the economic cost of these 'subsidies'. Are they perhaps not, like climate change, the price of un-costed elements coming back to haunt us? If so, you have to appreciate the extreme irony. After all, this industry is a primary contributor to climate change, not least because of the numbers of vehicles on the road – all resulting from the dubious selling practices!

Banking is not as volatile as the motor trade, nor does it have the same competitive challenges. So traditional banking profits generally only decline or disappear during a recession. Consequently the scale of the industry's bailouts is an even bigger indictment of the way these businesses have been managed and/or their accounting. They certainly suggest past profits were likely overstated or else inappropriately distributed. Even more annoying is that they also indicate that past bonuses have been overpaid and were unjustified. (Ironically there seem to have been no consequences whatsoever for the managers responsible, who, by and large, have been left running the businesses – albeit for new shareholders: the taxpayer. This is a blatant example of the lack of accountability that I wrote about earlier.)

UNACCOUNTED COSTS

You may recall that, apart from drawing an analogy with Newton's 3rd Law of Motion, I cited climate change as *the* classic example of true costs not being accounted for at the time and the bill we now face for trying to save the environment as being the unrecognised costs associated with past profits. This could affect any number of industries, but the most obvious ones to have effectively reported false or over-inflated profits would be:

- The oil companies;
- The energy companies;
- The transport industry (in its widest sense); etc.

Interestingly, as awareness of the environmental damage has increased, so efforts have been made to account for some of these costs. For example, quarry companies have been expected to restore the landscape and remove the scars that they would formerly have left. Also mining companies and others have been expected to make reparation for any damage they may have caused. Oil spills are the prime example here. Yet even here commercial interests have prevailed and nothing like the full costs have ever been accounted for or paid. Certainly, if you take the case of logging or farming in the Amazon it is doubtful whether those companies ever could.

Often local economic interests take precedence over wider economic interests. Companies are able to convince politicians and others they are actually doing good by creating jobs and raising the standard of living of the area.

As a result there is little new here. The major industrial nations even look to paint a picture of the good work they are doing in this area by creating a system of trading pollution whereby the worst polluters, those who are failing to meet agreed standards, can purchase credits from the good guys who are exceeding them.

THE PEOPLE JUSTIFICATION

It is particularly ironic that so much of what is questionable is justified on the economic grounds that it provides jobs and/or raises living standards in the area. Yet these companies will immediately look to make people redundant as soon as the commercial prospects don't look so good. However, this not only understates the true costs of doing business in the manner I described earlier, but also effectively transfers these costs to the community, in one or more of:

- Benefit payments;

- Lower trading as the result of lower discretionary spending;

- Increased social costs through the psychological and health costs and/or the impact on the person laid off and their dependents;

- Increased crime by the really desperate.

Exacerbating the effects of the downturn, making it deeper and more long lasting than it would otherwise be, this is simply organisational self-interest. It can be likened to the crew manning the lifeboats and leaving passengers on a sinking ship to fend for themselves.

It is particularly obnoxious in companies operating in a cyclical industry, such as the motor trade or construction, which is normally amongst the first affected by any economic downturn. So it certainly adds insult to injury when the motor industry asks the government to bail them out. That is effectively going to the well twice.

In the light of all this, the rationale for bailing out the banks is questionable and considering it for the motor industry is even more so. I make no great claims to understand the economics, but it seems clear to me that a whole lot of money has disappeared on things that have no value and consequently the world's wealth has shrunk considerably. There has to be a readjustment somewhere, and in that context one can only question whether the various governments' rescue efforts are politically rather than economically motivated. If so, are they not just delaying the inevitable?

Companies that make people redundant fail to live up to the spirit of Roosevelt's words and put evanescent profits above all else. This is also ironic when it doesn't really help in the long-term, and they take longer to snap back after a recession than those that don't do so.

Such behaviour sends out a message that people are not important. It is thus humiliating and does nothing for their sense of self-worth. It also does little to motivate them to work harder or to show any loyalty to their employer. That company described earlier that makes a million profit one year and a half a million loss the next pays dividends and bonuses in the first year, based solely on that year's results. Consequently the recipients do very nicely, thank you. So those who are made redundant the next can hardly be blamed for feeling hard done by or thinking that the bosses are only looking after their own interests.

It should thus come as little surprise that the union members in the US motor manufacturers are against taking a salary cut in order to secure a bailout package. In an environment where the income gap has been steadily rising, it seems entirely logical that they will feel they are being asked to bear a proportionately greater share of the burden.

Thus treating people as assets has multiple benefits. It means that the philosophy "our people are our greatest asset" will be practised at both the micro and macro levels with greater consistency. This in turn will mean that:

- Companies will have to be more prudent in the way they employ people.

- Companies will have to bear the costs of the good times and bad themselves.

- Hidden people costs will no longer remain unaccounted for and the economic costs will be more accurately evaluated.

- Business models will improve and government will not be called upon to make questionable bailouts.

- Recessions will be shorter and less hurtful to the community than they would otherwise have been.

All this is possible because valuing people as assets begins to shift the focus away from profit to value. It brings a more balanced value-added approach to business, fitting in with 'the value motive' propounded by Kearns whilst also aligning with his point, *'Maximum value can only be achieved by maximising the value of people.'* It offers an organisational development solution that provides an alternative to the historical command and control management style, while at the same time appealing to the traditionalists by incorporating the measurement capability to assess the results of these new initiatives, and so ensure that control is not totally lost.

Most significantly of all, however, it will start to deliver on Roosevelt's words. It will build a work environment where there is "the joy of achievement and the thrill of creative effort" and people will all have a much greater sense of self-worth.

CHAPTER TEN

Managing Government Finances

"Faced with a crisis, the man of character falls back on himself. He imposes his own stamp of action, takes responsibility for it, makes it his own."

CHARLES DE GAULLE

The fulcrum of any debate between capitalist and socialist is the role of government. The capitalist decries state interference and tries to minimise the role of government. On the other hand, the socialist decries the self-interest of the capitalist and maintains that a strong central government is necessary in order to look after the greater good of the community.

It is therefore a very strange quirk of fate that has seen the demise of capitalism in the US, the bastion of world capitalism, ushered in by a governing party and a president elected to champion its principles. Yet, the government bailouts of the financial services companies and the motor trade have effectively done that. They have effectively let the genie out of the bottle and it is unlikely that it can ever be put back. I wrote earlier about the convergence of capitalist and socialist doctrines and the growth of central government. This is perhaps the biggest single example of that phenomenon.

At this point I had a quote by Karl Marx that I wanted to include, in which he appeared to forecast the present financial crisis and how it would lead to the spreading of communism. Unfortunately, although it apparently has been posted more than 12 million times on the internet, I was unable to authenticate it and it may even be disputed, (a glaring example of how dangerous the internet can be as a source of information) and so - rather than risk being guilty of compounding the dissemination of false information - I decided it would be unethical to use it.

Nevertheless, something Marx did say which is relevant is, *'While the miser is merely a capitalist gone mad, the capitalist is a rational miser.'* There is clearly a great danger when the bounds of rationality get crossed and the capitalist becomes a miser. Even Henry Ford recognised this when he stated, *'A business that makes nothing but money is a poor kind of business.'* This occurs when making profits becomes the exclusive focus of business, and it appears to have been one of the primary causes of the credit crunch that caused the current economic downturn.

Certainly, the manner in which business leaders turned to government to bail them out of the mess of their own making makes a mockery of their proclaimed values. It is difficult to take anyone seriously who proclaims the right of the market to operate unfettered, and of business to make its own way and let the market be the ultimate judge of performance, when they appeal for government rescue when the market finds them wanting. As we saw in the last chapter, business has played a very major part in its own downfall.

Of course the situation is not confined to the US. The interconnection of a global economy also required other governments to intervene. The scale of these bailouts places an extremely heavy burden on these governments – and the taxpayers who fund all their activity. It also comes at a very bad time for governments when, as we saw previously, the demands on their exchequers continue to increase. Of course this is worse during a recession when tax revenues are reduced, but is further complicated by governments having limited scope to raise revenues as a result of their already significant share of national GDP. If the government stake in the economy gets much bigger we are almost certain to be worse off in the longer-term, unless we can find a way to make government more efficient.

Thus both the private and public sectors are going to have to think and act outside the box if we are not to be like frogs and perish in waters that are starting to get unbearably hot. Needless to say I have a couple of ideas on the subject.

TAX EFFICIENCY

You may recall that I have a number of issues with our tax system. Very broadly these include the fact:

- Corporation tax basically subsidises the inefficient.

- Tax revenues are used too much as an instrument of policy.

- The tax system is unnecessarily complex.

- Collection is unwieldy and the costs disproportionate to the revenues obtained.

It may be useful here for me to recapitulate the point about corporate tax subsidising the inefficient. Not only is this key to my whole proposed solution, but it also provides a strong thread that ties in with many other issues raised.

Not only is the method of calculating corporate profit questionable for all the reasons I have already explained, but to use it as a basis for corporation tax is illogical. It effectively means that government (and hence you and I as taxpayers) effectively subsidise inefficient business. As I wrote before, "Businessmen in any economy, capitalist or socialist, work to maximise profit, which simply means doing everything possible to maximise sale and reduce costs. The bigger the profit, the more successful a business is considered. And all other things being equal, the greater the tax the business pays ... Other companies may compete in the same market, offering exactly the same services but not making the same profits. Why not? Quite simply, because their managers are not as efficient i.e. they cannot generate sales or reduce costs to the same level. As a result these companies are not required to pay as much tax. … The natural corollary to this is that inefficient business is benefiting from being inefficient and is thus being subsidised."

Perhaps an example will make this point clearer. Let us assume that two businessmen need to attend a conference in New York and have to fly there from London. Hardly surprisingly, they end up on the same flight. However, one flies first class for (say) £5,000 while the second flies economy for (say) £250. Since the objective of a business is to make a profit, this by definition means the second is more efficient than the first - in this example 20 times more efficient. In both case these flights constitute a legitimate business expense and so are allowable for tax purposes. This means that they reduce their company profits by £5,000 and £250 respectively. Thus, because corporation tax is levied on profit each has reduced their tax base by that amount. Let's now assume a corporation tax rate of 20%. This means that the former company will pay £1000 less tax, while the latter will pay £50 less tax. This means that you and I as tax-payers have effectively contributed those amounts to their respective businesses. Clearly then we have subsided the inefficient to a greater extent than we have subsidised the efficient.

Now you might buy in to the argument that the first businessman would make; namely that flying first class allows him to work better on the plane, arrive more refreshed and better able to deal with the issues that arise at the conference, etc, etc. That might well be the case, but it doesn't alter the fact that as taxpayer we have contributed to his creature comforts. But if you need a more extreme example, just think about all the bonuses paid to the city bankers. These are also business expenses and so are tax-deductible. So for every £1 million bonus we are effectively contributing £200K! Even if, assuming that the individual concerned hasn't found a way to ensure the receipt is tax sheltered and thus not susceptible to income tax or else is taxed at a considerably reduced rate, this is offset by the fact that this is now taxable in the individual's hands, the principle is questionable. Would the businesses pay such large bonuses if they were not tax deductible?

Surely I cannot be alone in thinking this is absolute lunacy? And, any response that it has to be like this because there is no other alternative doesn't wash with me either. For a species that has been demonstrating unprecedented levels of intelligence for over 4000 years we have to be able to come up with a better answer than that!

For my part I am suggesting a relatively simple three part solution. This would be to introduce:

1.   A flat rate tax charged on revenue. This would apply universally to individuals and corporations alike and apply to all primary income or sales. In business terms this means a top-line tax instead of a bottom-line tax.

2.   The elimination of tax allowances and the segregation of collection and disbursement functions. This means that there would be no 'tax credits' or other convoluted schemes to reduce taxes collected. Instead any attempts to mitigate tax must be recognised as the policy decision it really is, and made through the disbursement of money by the relevant arm of government.

3.   As far as practically possible, value based charges for all government services. This would be used to offset the costs of running government services, and so leave tax revenues for national expenditures such as policing, defence, etc.

RATIONALE

It is hopefully self-evident that this solution will be considerably more simple than the current systems and thus offer greater ease of use and a more cost-effective approach. However, there are additional factors that make it attractive, not only in the current economic climate, but also as a solution to the challenges ahead.

Firstly, taxing on the top-line rather than the bottom-line allows a considerably lower tax rate to be applied. This will reduce the tendency to want to cheat on paying taxes that is currently so endemic. This will allow greater flexibility and create more scope to find the programmes needed to address global warming and the other such challenges that lie ahead.

Secondly it will allow taxes to be collected sooner as with PAYE and VAT and so, by improving government cashflows, reduce the amount of tax that needs to be raised.

Thirdly, it will bring government revenues more into line with the prevailing economy and reduce the impact of recession on tax collections. Tax collection on the basis of profit means that tax revenues decline dramatically during a recession, when business generally makes less profit and many organisations actually make losses. By changing the basis to a sales figure governments are eliminating a large proportion of that effect. Yes, their revenues will be lower than normal but the impact will only be the same as it is for the business sector and not multiplied by the effect on profits.

As a result, in difficult economic times like the ones we are currently experiencing, the impact on government will be reduced and so government will need to borrow less to make up the shortfall. Consequently the economy as a whole will bounce back that much sooner and be better prepared to take advantage of a return to good times.

Finally, it also offers a means to reduce the government share of GDP. This will foster economic development and allow the economy to grow much faster than it otherwise would. At the same time, this will allow taxpayers to get more involved in economic development and/or community work; to feel that they are making a greater contribution and thus improve their sense of self-worth.

JUSTIFICATION AND BENEFITS

If that is not justification enough, I am more than confident that this solution would address all four of my points above and some others as well, but let me make the case more cogently and address any obvious objections.

Subsidising the Inefficient

This approach clearly puts an end to government effectively penalising efficient businesses and subsidising inefficient ones. It:

- Creates a level playing field that all businessmen and entrepreneurs should welcome.

- Enables businesses to focus more on their operational effectiveness without wasting time on tax matters and/or their implications.

- Simplifies investor analysis and facilitates better comparison between businesses both in and across market sectors.

- Ensures greater economic efficiency as businesses would no longer be able to use tax incentives or exploit tax 'loopholes' for operations.

Tax as an Instrument of Policy

For too long tax has had a debilitating effect on economic performance. As an instrument of policy it has been a means of distorting the operation of the market and contributed to the misuse of economic resources. I have voiced reservations about the effectiveness of the markets for governing economic activity, but this is mainly because of humankind's remarkable ability to act like silly moths around a flame. This is only too evident from the kinds of excesses that have recently come to light. However, these have been as much the result of the failure of proper enforcement of regulations as the failure to use common sense.

The market remains fundamentally the best vehicle to shape economic development, but in order to do this it requires:

- A government whose number one responsibility is to ensure and facilitate the efficient use of economic resources and to police their use.

- Proper enforcement of regulations and oversight of that enforcement.

- More effective comparative analysis of companies in the same market sector with the immediate review if one's performance outstrips the others by more than a given percentage.

- Measures to ensure that the market cannot be manipulated by either too powerful investors or investors acting in collusion. This could be achieved amongst other things by:

- Eliminating or placing more stringent controls on derivatives, futures and any other non-discrete financial product. Certainly one of the problems with the banking system is that the nature of option dealing is such that it is actually a form of financial wagering. The industry should confine itself to only dealing in 'tangible' products that its clients can readily understand, ensuring that there is no additional risk other than what is intrinsic to the product itself and the market.

- Restricting the size of trades by any particular trader or business over any specified period.

- Restricting the volume or percentage holding of any particular share that can be traded over any given period by one shareholder, and the ability to buy and sell on the same day.

- More stringent penalties for anyone who tries to manipulate the market.

- Greater reinforcement of ethics and ethical standards. This could be achieved, amongst other things, by:
  - More stringent penalties for unethical or corrupt behaviour.
  - Diluting the power that any individual business leader can exert.

Of course I have to get a plug in here and add that my proposal to make the people working for a company all co-owners would go a long way towards reducing the risk of executive malfeasance on the recent scale. This will be even stronger if they have the long-term perspective that I have proposed by suggesting their ownership also forms part of their pension plan.

Removing Complexity

This has to be a major benefit of this proposal. It effectively eliminates thousands of pages of tax law and the guidelines and interpretations all at once and replaces them with something that is conceptually so simple a schoolchild could understand it.

Once the initial implementation is complete, it will also release the intellectual capabilities of all the tax lawyers and advisors, and enable them to apply their abilities to something that is more economically productive. This may sound very high-handed, but I also believe that in the long run it will contribute to a greater sense of self worth.

Of course I cannot really take credit for this idea. It originates in the concept of tithing. It has thus been around for millennia and proves the adage that there is nothing new under the sun. However, it worked for the ancient Romans and there is no law that says that, just because we have computers we have to make everything more complicated.

Reducing Collection Costs

This approach will substantially reduce the costs, including:

- Preparation time and costs.
- Query costs.
- Inspection and investigation costs.
- Penalty and prosecution costs.

There is also the wonderful thought that it will replace VAT or conventional Sales Taxes. However, from a business perspective it is actually not very far removed from a sales tax. Thus it offers the additional attraction, while eliminating the complexity and irritation that goes with those taxes, it will be able to utilise much of their administrative infrastructure thus should be relatively easy to implement.

Inequity

One of the biggest philosophical issues with existing income tax is the question of varying rates. On one hand the humanitarians argue that it is only right that those who earn more should pay tax at a higher rate. On the other hand those of a more conservative persuasion argue that those who earn more, by virtue of that very fact, make a greater economic contribution already and that it is thus inappropriate for them to pay a higher rate.

Consistent with my earlier point that higher taxes discourage community involvement, I am inclined to fall into the latter camp. I thus believe that a single flat rate is entirely fair. Democracy is based on the principle of equality, and on that basis gives every adult a single vote. Accordingly it is entirely equitable that every individual should pay tax at the same rate.

I hope and expect that this would to some extent be compensated for by the higher earners doing more charitable giving. Even if this is not the case, though, I would still not change my opinion. One of the idiosyncrasies of income tax, proved by Reaganomics and the lower tax regimes introduced by Reagan and Thatcher is that lower rates result in higher tax collections. I believe there are two reasons for this:

1. The obvious resentment of higher taxes.

2. Resentment of the way the tax is spent (squandered?)

Higher earners are often more money motivated and consequently they see a financial reward in doing everything they possibly can to reduce the amount of tax they pay.

Thus, a single, lower flat rate will reduce all these factors. To ensure that, and drive the message home that cheating on tax is unethical and unacceptable behaviour I would also consider making the penalties for doing so more onerous. I believe this disincentive is sufficient.

Redistribution of Wealth

One of the purposes often assigned to tax is "the redistribution of wealth". The thinking here is that tax is necessary in order to help the poor and disadvantaged to achieve a better standard of living. This is fundamentally socialist philosophy and assumes:

- Those with the wealth are incapable of helping the poor without any coercion to do so.

- Government can do a better job in this regard than can the private sector.

This is a largely spurious position.

It is only true if government looks upon this role as being an investing role. That requires a closer alignment with the basic philosophy of Moses Maimonides, who in the 12th century said that, *"The noblest charity is to preclude a man from accepting charity, and the best alms are to show and enable a man to dispense with alms"*. There is certainly no evidence of any such philosophy here in Britain. Nor does any change seem likely, although it is interesting, in recent weeks, to see a

146

Labour (socialist) government starting to make noises about clamping down on long-term benefit payments.

It is not a coincidence that charitable giving in the UK is proportionately lower than in the US. This is, I believe, the result of British people increasingly regarding helping the disadvantaged as a government role and the taxes they pay as their contribution to the cause. In discussing this earlier, I also described how the welfare state with its system of social benefits has created a monster, with a second generation of dependency by people who make little or no contribution to society at all. This system has thus been self-defeating and has created succeeding generations with little or no sense of self-worth and the ghastly consequences that breeds.

This all increases the demands on government which in turn is making it increasingly difficult to fund. I suspect it is these fiscal constraints more than any recognition of the system's philosophical shortcomings, which are prompting the government rethink. But, either way the system is going to have to change, and the solutions proposed here will provide a good platform for doing so. They recognise the failure of both capitalism and socialism and so compel a fresh approach that will:

- Acknowledge government's limited capability to provide the same sort of economic stimulation as the private sector and limit or change its capabilities accordingly.

- Recognise the need to invest in people rather than simply provide an income stream and develop a system to deliver this.

Alternative Sources of Revenue

One of the hot issues in recent British politics has been the proliferation of "stealth taxes" – new ways for the government to raise money. A single, flat rate of tax should provide a strong enough basis to eliminate this. Government revenues should be confined to the following:

- Personal income tax – calculated on a flat rate against personal earnings from paid remuneration, pensions, annuities and rental income.

- Corporation tax – calculated on a flat rate based on sales or activities that are deemed to be sales.

- Duties and excises on imported goods and tobacco, alcoholic beverages and drugs.

- Proceeds from the provision of services – as far as possible on a realistic, economic cost basis.

- Penalties and fines from non-compliance with legislation or regulations.

Note that VAT and Sales Taxes are not included in the list. These are specifically excluded as they are too complicated and costly to implement and/or enforce. The whole point here is to restrict what the government can do and to compel them to administer all this considerably better than they do at present. To ensure this the following fundamental principles would be enshrined in law to prevent the system being abused.

- There will be no taxes on income that has already been taxed. This used to be enshrined in law and has been eroded over time as governments have become increasingly anxious to identify more sources of revenue.

- There will be no taxes on interest on savings or loans (unless it is part of an individual's or organisation's regular business) or on dividends (including labour dividends as described earlier).

- There would be no capital gains or inheritance tax.

Greater Economic Effectiveness

The whole philosophy underlying everything outlined here, is that the world needs to manage its resources more efficiently.

In the last chapter we saw that even businesses do not necessarily do this and outlined proposals to rectify that. Here we are trying to achieve precisely the same thing.

Historically government expenditure has been notoriously inefficient and this needs to change. Accordingly all the solutions identified thus far, as well as those in the next section, are aimed at facilitating this change. A number of fundamental principles need to be enshrined in all law to ensure this:

- Government has overall supervisory and legislative powers to ensure that economic resources are properly used and all the related costs are identified and properly accounted for.

- Government is responsible for the administration and enforcement of procedures to ensure this.

- Government is constitutionally restricted to the proportion of GDP that it can raise in taxes, excises and duties.

- The tax rate is to be set at the lowest possible rate which will enable government to carry out its redefined role.

- Changes in that rate will have to be justified to parliament and approved by a two-thirds majority.

There is Only One Taxpayer

I have already written about my great epiphany: the fact that there is only one of me! The key thing about this is that it limits the contribution that I am able (or willing) to make to the national coffers. Of course I understand the need to pay taxes and recognise that choosing where I live brings obligations with it, and thus I am certainly prepared to pay my share. However, I have a problem doing so when:

- The rate seems unduly punitive.
- I am seeing my own standard of living falling.
- Government does not use what it collects efficiently.

Consequently issues of the sort I described in Chapter 8 tend to make me rather grumpy, especially when the recent challenges of rapidly rising food, energy and fuel prices are having a definite downward pull on our standard of living. In such circumstances it seems iniquitous that a young sixteen year old can go out and get herself pregnant and, as a reward for her sins, be given a free house, which you and I are effectively helping pay for. It is hardly surprising, then, that Britain has the highest teen pregnancy rate in Europe - it is called reinforcing negative behaviour!

Yet somehow none of our political leaders or public administrators can see the connection. The battle cry of reducing poverty and particularly child poverty is chanted from city halls across the country and the cult of political correctness does the rest. Nowhere along the line does anyone learn that actions have consequences, and that these are not always pleasant. So instead what is effectively anti-social behaviour gets positively reinforced and these young girls, low on self-esteem and desperate for affection and someone in their lives who will love them unconditionally, persist. In fact they learn that they will get even more benefits if they repeat the exercise and so we breed a society of Karen Matthewses.

Now the government is talking about withdrawing their benefits if these girls don't get themselves a job by the time the child turns two. Has no-one explained the law of unintended consequences to them and pointed out that this will simply reinforce the need to keep on having children? Or the likelihood of this resulting in Dickensian type squalor rather than eliminating child poverty? Of course this process will be accelerated as we all end up in penury paying for it.

This sense that the lunatics are running the asylum is exacerbated by the government's efforts to pay for it all. No-one seems to understand that it is me who pays:

- The income tax.
- The national insurance.
- The VAT on nearly everything I buy.
- The Council Tax.
- The Fuel Tax every time I fill up my car.
- The Car Licence.
- The TV Licence.

Come to think about it, in light of all this it is hardly surprising that employee engagement is a problem. Most of us who are employed are increasingly wondering what the point of it all is and wondering whether we too should quit our jobs and simply live off benefits. Maybe we would be even better off if we went out and committed a felony so that we could end up in jail. While overcrowding is starting to become a problem at least that way we would get free accommodation, three good meals a day, the chance to watch as much television as we like, read books and even smoke the odd joint. Who knows it might even increase the odds of winning the lottery.

Lest you think I am being facetious, the following report from "The Times" indicates that prison officers are claiming that prisoners are actually breaking in to prisons because they miss the life so much. I kid you not!

June 4, 2008

Prisoners Turning Down The Chance Of Early Release

Thousands treat it as 'state-run B&B lodging'

Francis Elliott, Deputy Political Editor

Britain's jails will be criticised today as no more than costly bed-and-break-fast lodgings as new figures show that thousands of prisoners a year reject the chance of early release.

More than 37,000 inmates opted out of tagging and other release schemes between 1999 and 2006, Jack Straw, the Justice Secretary, admitted yesterday. He also revealed that 42 people have been caught trying to break into prisons in the past five years.

The figures add weight to claims that jail has become an attractive option for many inmates. Gordon Brown, fearful of being seen as soft on crime, stepped in recently to block a planned pay rise for prisoners.

He took action after a warning by Glyn Travis, assistant general secretary of the Prison Officers' Association, that inmates were reluctant to leave because drugs were now cheaper in jail.

Nick Herbert, the Shadow Justice Secretary, who obtained the new figures in a series of parliamentary answers, said that they laid bare Labour's "farcical mismanagement" of the prison system. "How secure are our jails if criminals can break into them? Whether these are offenders trying to return to jail, as prison officers have alleged, or dealers trying to traffic drugs, it is ludicrous that supposedly secure establishments can be breached in this way."

However, the Ministry of Justice said that breakins at closed prisons were extremely rare and also challenged the claim that prisoners opted out of being considered for tagging and other early-release schemes because they wanted to stay inside. "Among the most likely reasons are that the prisoner cannot provide details of a release address or will consider that it is highly unlikely he or she will pass the risk assessment and does not bother to apply," a spokesman said.

Business leaders will heap further criticism on the criminal justice system today at a CBI conference. Neil Bentley, director of public services, is expected to say that prison is being "used as a hugely expensive bed-and-breakfast facility that keeps criminals out of circulation". He will add that reoffending rates show the "colossal failure" of existing criminal justice policies with two in three people who go through prison being convicted of another crime within two years of release, rising to three in four among young offenders.

"If two in three pupils left school unable to read or write, or two in three patients left their GP surgery as in need of medical attention as when they went in, the reaction would be one of anger, and rightly so," Dr Bentley will say.

The CBI estimated recently that the annual cost of crime was £60 billion, about 5 per cent of Brtain's GDP.

A Ministry of Justice spokesman said: "It is ridiculous to conflate these two issues. Prison is anything but soft and it is absurd to suggest otherwise.

"The punishment of the court is loss of liberty by being sent to prisons which combine tough regimes with the opportunity of rehabilitation.

"While trespass into open prisons is more difficult to control, there has only been one identified case of a member of the public breaking into a closed prison in the last five years."

And, just in case you are inclined to believe the men from the ministry here is another report which indicates the problem is not unique to Britain.

Ex-Con Tries To Break Back Into Jail

A young Austrian convict missed prison so much after his release that he tried to break back in.

Detlef Federsohn, 23, was released from the Josefstadt prison in the Austrian capital Vienna after serving two years for theft.

But he was arrested last week when police were called out to a suspected prison break after he was spotted on the roof of the jail.

Federsohn said: "Life is so much easier on the inside. They feed you, do your washing and let you watch TV, which I can tell you is a lot more than my mum does. So I thought if I could sneak back in I would blend in with the others and the screws wouldn't notice."

If this is not proof that the world has gone crazy I don't know what is. As one letter-writer wrote in response to the Times, *"If life is better on the inside than the outside, it is the outside that needs fixing."* Amen!

As I say, (getting back on track) every attempt of the government to pay for this ultimately comes back to you and me. It is no good government boasting that they have managed to hold income tax rates steady when my local council rates have gone up 5%, or when I am paying £1.27 a litre for petrol and something like 64% of that is going directly to their pockets.

My earlier suggestion that there should be just one single flat rate of tax goes some way towards redressing this. But even more needs to be done to ensure that taxes are set on the principle that the absolute burden to the individual taxpayer is known.

This is becoming increasingly important because, despite the increasing costs of government, the layers of government are actually increasing. I mentioned previously the situation in Canada where there is:

- Municipal government,

- Regional government,

- Provincial government,

- National government.

However, it is not so different in Britain where, county councils equate to regional government and, although there is no provincial government, there is a strong movement to introduce regional government. To some extent this is to counteract the effect in England of the fact that Scotland, Wales and Northern Ireland all have their own parliaments with all the ceremony, bureaucracy and pomp that goes with them.

The trend here mirrors what we have seen in Europe. The great paradox is that the more we try to centralise power in a stronger central government, the more nationalism raises it head. This is symptomised by the break up of the Balkans as well as the former Soviet Union, and to some extent reflects the natural desire each of us has to control our own destiny, as epitomised by de Gaulle's words at the beginning of the chapter.

On the other hand globalisation, together with the environmental issues the world faces, means there is a growing need for greater cohesion with agreed policies and concerted action to deliver them. This creates a dichotomy with forces moving in two opposite directions. The net effect is that this is likely to leave us with the following layers of government all of which have to be paid for one way or another.

- Municipal government (Village, town and city).

- Regional government (County or its replacement if we do away with the historical boundaries).

- National government (NEWS – Northern Ireland, England, Wales & Scotland[27]).

- Federal government (United Kingdom or Great Britain[28]).

- State government (European Union).

Self-interest at the lowest ('local') level makes it difficult enough to achieve any sort of consensus about how to proceed for the greater good of the planet. But it isn't going to be any easier to achieve if we continue with these multiple layers of government, each adding its own costs and effectively taking productive capacity from the economy.

This is unquestionably one of the most fundamental issues of our times, but it remains one that is not openly debated. It is a classic example of an issue that is heating the water yet being ignored. The whole European Union remains a divisive issue partly because the ultimate intention and rationale is not fully understood. The community's scope has expanded since it was first formed and many are dubious as to the end goal. Remember, two world wars were fought in part to avoid creating a single state Europe and it is therefore inevitable that current efforts will be perceived as an attempt to do so 'via

---

[27] Ironically this would be likely to guarantee the ultimate unification of Ireland and so negate "the troubles" and the tragic loss of life they caused through most of the 20th Century.

[28] This may also well disappear if each of the constituent countries does go its own way, with the loss of the history and the international political and economic 'clout' that has gone with it.

the back door'. Opposition will only be overcome if and when politicians come clean and explain the rationale for it, how it will be afforded and the democratic shortcoming described earlier dealt with.

I am convinced that part of the problem is that this structure is inverted. The concept of a large central government is a fundamental contradiction of the principles of democracy. Thus the pyramid and certainly the government revenue structures – and hence the tax structures – are inverted. There are undoubtedly valid historical reasons for this but, going back to the dirty painting analogy, these have perhaps become lost in the passage of time. And, while the cost of creating the systems to oversee this needed to have been borne by a larger, more centralised body, this may also no longer be valid.

Therefore I suggest that tax should be collected from the individual at the community level, and the community should be responsible for contributing to the next levels on a fixed percentage basis. Thus local government would collect tax from the individuals and businesses in that community on the fixed percentage basis described previously. It would then pay a fixed proportion of the tax collected to the next level or each of the next levels.

In other words each level would effectively pay a fixed rate tax to the next level. Thus assuming hypothetically for a moment the historic concept of tithing would apply:

- The individual or business would pay 10% of their gross earnings (sales).

- The local government would then pay 10% of that to the regional government.

- The regional government would then pay 10% to the national government.

- The national government would then pay 10% to the federal government.

- The federal government would then pay 10% to the state government.

There would be a number of benefits to such a scheme. Let's have a look at what some of the might be.

Grass Roots Democracy

This will truly restore democracy to its basic principles. People will be far closer to the decisions that affect their everyday lives and thus take far greater interest. The increased importance of local government elections will reduce the current apathy that surrounds them and rekindle greater involvement by the community.

Greater Accountability

With local government no longer being the bottom rung of the government ladder, government officers can no longer point a finger at others (including central government) when things go wrong. Officials will have to perform better not just because of the increased responsibility but also because their performance will be more closely scrutinised and by more people. Citizens will be better able to hold its elected officials accountable.

Reduced Corruption

Corporate governance will now be a fulltime occupation and call for greater professionalism. Now people will be elected for their capabilities rather than their political convictions and the calibre of local politicians will improve. This should also eliminate the need for party politics at this level. Arguably, introducing party politics to local government has been the single biggest cause of corruption. Voting along party lines embeds cronyism and a system of favours that breeds corruption. Greater transparency with greater accountability will also reduce this.

Improved Quality of Life

With local government being at the top of the totem pole instead of the bottom, more effort and more resources will be spent on the people in the community. This will enable core political and social issues to be addressed far more effectively than they currently are.

Greater Community Involvement

Greater community responsibility also means there will be less tolerance of slackers. The welfare scroungers and others of their ilk will simply not be tolerated to the extent they currently are, simply because the costs are being borne directly by the local community and not central government.

Greater Community Pride

With all of the above people will once again start taking more pride in their communities. Municipal workers will be more motivated and the standard of their work will improve. There will also generally be a greater community spirit with people willing to tackle issues rather than shrug shoulders and blame 'the government'.

More Efficient Use of Economic Resources

One of the supposed advantages of central government is that, like mass production, it is supposed to bring economies of scale. The problem is that getting resources to where they need to be often simultaneously creates greater waste. With the people affected having more accountability this will no longer be a problem.

Shared Resources

The drive for efficiency will also ensure greater co-operation between different communities. Thus rather than each investing in, say, a hospital they will look to share the investment and find a way that makes it suitable and convenient for both. This may for example result in increased costs for an ambulance shuttle from the community which doesn't have it, but overall this will still be a more efficient use of resources.

Outsourcing

I appreciate that this word may have negative connotations for many people but what I mean by this is simply that a community might not decide it wants to offer a particular service within that community. It can therefore simply elect to pay another community that does. A good example here would be a prison. A community that does not wish to have a prison can simply pay one that already has the amenities to administer its prisoners on its behalf. The key here is that the community has to *pay* for the privilege. Thus, for every one of its citizens convicted of a crime it has to pay the full cost of the upkeep of that convict, as well as the prosecution costs, to the respective communities that incur them. The principle here is that the community will ultimately bear the costs of its failure to build a crime free society and not just fob these costs off.

Reduced Importance of National Boundaries

A by-product of this scheme will be greater collaboration between neighbouring geographical communities. National boundaries, which are in any case arbitrary historical anomalies, will thus become less and less significant over time. So the nationalistic tendencies they create will hopefully then also diminish, and remove one of the primary causes of so much human conflict and misery.

Higher Level Governments

The next level governments will clearly have reduced roles. These will likely reduce even more over time as all the above begin to take effect but will include:

- Providing a central service organisation for the services that all these communities require. For example census and tax data, etc.

- Providing the larger scale infrastructure that the communities cannot build for themselves such as non-municipal roads, railways, etc.

- Overseeing the environmental needs and the standards needed to protect these and monitoring compliance with these.

- Energy policy and commissioning of energy services.

- Defence.

- International relations, etc.

The list is not intended to be exhaustive but simply to give an insight into what these other levels of government will do.

You will notice that the list includes defence. This recognises both history and the existing state of world affairs. However, I have to point out here that war has to be the single biggest contributor to waste, inefficient use of economic resources and the biggest risk to the environment. I thus hope that this new approach to government will shift priorities to such an extent as to make the cost of defence unaffordable and over time completely unnecessary.

Idealistic? Certainly. Naïve? Maybe. Possible? Definitely! Necessary? I would say so! That water is already getting too hot and it will be the only way to ensure we don't end up getting boiled alive.

The fact that capitalism and socialism have both failed so dramatically means we have to find a new way. At the same time the bills are too great for us to afford in our current state or with our existing model. We have to change and this is certainly a way that will enable all nations to come together, wipe the slate clean and start afresh. I don't think we can do much else. This proposal eliminates the massive innate inefficiencies of the existing systems of government, and builds on the individual in the way the founders of democracy first intended.

Moliere said, *"It is not only for what we do that we are held responsible, but also for what we do not do."* This gives us a platform to move forward to redress our past sins of omission and commission.

CHAPTER ELEVEN

Additional Thoughts

"Man must cease attributing his problems to his environment, and learn again to exercise his will and his personal responsibility."

ALBERT SCHWEITZER

Over the course of this book I have described how humankind has got into a way of thinking that simply builds on the past without reworking and challenging the assumptions that underpin our every day behaviour. I have described some of the fundamental social, economic and political issues that we face today that have their origins in this, and how our oblivion to this fact is analogous to the frog in hot water that allows itself to be boiled alive.

In doing so, I have stuck to an underlying theme that the modern generation is perhaps more self-centred and self-absorbed than any in history. Consequently, despite advances and developments that bring us comforts our ancestors could only dream of, we seem to be more discontented. This can be attributed to the erosion of the feel good factor that ultimately comes from doing things that help or please others. I have argued that we lack consideration for others in part because we have abrogated responsibility and leave too much to government. This socialistic creep, while well-intentioned, has had a debilitating effect on our ability to look out for others and to take responsibility for ourselves when things go wrong. In other words we have been running completely counter to the spirit of Schweitzer's words.

In the last two chapters I put forward suggestions as to how these problems could be systemically solved. Chapter 9 describes my ideas as to how to solve this problem in the commercial world, and Chapter 10 describes ideas as to how to solve them in the public sector. Both propositions ultimately focus on restoring personal accountability and creating a greater feeling of self-worth. Thus I would like to think that these solutions go some way towards meeting the standard Schweitzer set us.

However, the accountability issue is more fundamental and has more widespread implications. I simply cannot help thinking that many of society's wider ills stem from too much emphasis on rights and not enough on the concomitant obligations. Rights and responsibility are inseparable and we simply delude ourselves if we think we can have rights without any responsibility. Yet, increasingly, this seems to be the expectation, and it is typified by the lottery mentality where people pursue unrealistic wealth without ever having to earn it or, as research of winners seems to indicate, the faintest idea of how to manage when it is achieved. Other symptoms include minimally talented people entering talent shows and then turning aggressive and nasty when "their lives are ruined" by rejection; or - more recently - the 'bonus culture' that has clearly distorted both values and ethics.

Interestingly, during the time I have been writing, it seems that events have caused a shift in general thinking, and many of the things I have been writing about have moved more into the mainstream consciousness. Perhaps this is the dawning recognition of the rising water temperature. Of course the economic downturn has played a major part here, but it runs deeper than that. Now there is also open discussion about a 'broken society' although, unfortunately, much of the debate centres around the term and its validity, rather than the means for repairing it.

This encourages me to think that there is an audience out there for new ideas. It also emboldens me, on the basis of Einstein's principle that a problem cannot be solved from the same level of consciousness that created it, to comment on matters where I have little or no direct personal experience. My thoughts and opinions are subjective, based simply on reports that I have read, seen or heard. Nevertheless these reports are worrying and, I believe, they do point to a society that, if not broken, is breaking. I believe better education about accountability would be a significant first step to repairing it, and if the following ideas have any merit and could contribute towards this I shall be well pleased.

THE PRINCIPLE OF CONSEQUENCES

Labouring the point about accountability and consequences may seem contradictory to the philosophy of encouraging self-worth. Yet accountability is a key element for changing behaviour and consequences are an essential facet of teaching accountability. This is something past generations clearly understood but which we somehow appear to have forgotten.

Actions have consequences. If I go out for a meal and eat too much, I suffer the discomfort of having done so. There is a direct connection between the two events. Similarly, if I bend down to pick up a book that my cat has knocked off my desk, get up too soon and bump my head, that too is a consequence of *my* action. I cannot blame anyone but myself - even if I do curse the cat. (In fact I often find that it is when I am cursing the cat or the equivalent that I do something like bump my head!) Another example could be slipping into a shop quickly without putting money in the meter and ending up getting a parking ticket. In this case I incur a penalty - a consequence imposed by someone else - but it is still a direct result of my action.

Consequences may be self-inflicted or imposed by someone else, be direct or indirect, but they are inevitability an outcome of our own actions and the choices we make. I cannot help wondering if we are failing to drive this basic lesson home to our children. How often today do we witness parents failing to follow through on their threats? "Johnny, I told you to stop doing that. If you don't stop, you'll have to go to your room. Johnny, I have asked you three times now. Please stop that! Oh, Johnny, you are naughty - you never do as you are told, do you?" Idle threats will never teach children this basic lesson.

Consequences, however, are by no means a complete solution as this delightful story illustrates.

A young father was very hot on the issue of consequences and wanted to ensure that he instilled it in his children. So he saw the problem of his 3-year-old son clobbering his younger brother as an ideal opportunity to do so. Accordingly he made it quite clear that it was the lad's choice as to whether he did it or not, but that if he did he would be sent to his room. Children being the masters of philosophy they are, the lad soon learned the lesson, but not quite in the way envisaged. One day he gave his brother a hefty thump, and then marched off, announcing, "Okay, I am going to my bedroom now!"

Apart from the obvious middle-class overtones of the story, the effectiveness or otherwise as a punishment of sending a child to its room could be the subject of a book in itself, and the story serves primarily to reinforce how difficult parenting can be. Clearly though, to be an effective deterrent, consequences have to be less desirable than the causative action!

PREVENTION BETTER THAN CURE

Of course, this story highlights the fact that consequences are predominantly a reactive agent in effecting change. In order to ensure the sort of behaviour where the older sibling does not thump junior requires more proactive agency. This is obviously more easily said than done, and I certainly don't profess to have all the answers. There is no doubt, though, that this begins with several basic steps:

1. Teaching young people from an early age that actions have consequences and that consequences are mostly the result of choice.

2. Doing more to encourage positive behaviour.

3. Doing more to make it clear that anti-social behaviour is unacceptable. While there is no place in modern society for an attitude that "children should be seen and not heard" there is equally no place for an attitude that children should be allowed to express themselves freely when this is at the expense of other people's rights.

There is a danger here of falling into the trap of traditional carrot and stick thinking, and assuming that consequences have to be stick, and proactive methods more carrot. Thus one almost inevitably thinks that points 1 and 3 are the former and point 2 the latter. This is probably the most likely scenario but does not necessarily have to be the case, and is the province that calls for more "out-of-the-box" thinking. The key is to identify proactive consequences; and this inevitably requires solutions that make people feel good about themselves when they do the right things.

COUNTERING ANTI-SOCIAL BEHAVIOUR

Earlier I described in some detail the problem with young, single mothers having additional children in order to continue getting benefits, and of prisoners being reluctant to leave, and even breaking back into, prison. This is the lightning rod that shows the extent to which the pendulum has swung too far. There are other signs too, such as the infamous Anti-Social Behaviour Disorders or ASBOs intended to discourage youngsters from anti-social or criminal behaviour, while sparing them jail terms (in already overcrowded prisons) but which reports indicate serve instead as a badge of honour.

While I have no first hand experience of these issues, reports increasingly leave me with the impression that the problem here is that we give undue consideration to the offenders' rights. In the process we add to our costs and, often, to the indignity and suffering of their victims. This isn't right. People who infringe on other people's human rights should forfeit some of their own, at least until such time as they can demonstrate they deserve to have them reinstated.

As an outsider it seems to me that our penal system is clearly not working effectively and provides neither retribution nor rehabilitation. It is okay not to focus on the old-fashioned retribution, but we need to balance the punishment and the rehabilitation aspects, and do more to ensure the latter. If we don't the system becomes pointless.

That is a key point. The criminal system is naturally, almost by definition, a consequence and thus is a predominantly reactive system; dealing with events after they happen. It is necessary, but – as any parent knows – it is preferable to prevent undesirable behaviour than to punish the offence afterwards. Consequently there has to be some sort of deterrent factor to prevent recurrence, but there also needs to be something in place to help the offender change their behaviour. At present the penal system seems to achieve neither. Prison is the adult equivalent of sending a naughty child to its room.

The first step to rectify this is to remove any impression that prison life is easy. This means that convicts should suffer some hardship and for starters being incarcerated should mean:

- Losing their democratic rights such as the right to vote;
- Losing their social rights, including:
  - The right to watch television,

- o The right to smoke or (incredible as it seems) to take recreational drugs,
- o The right to do normal everyday things like buying lottery tickets. Should they break this rule and happen to win (as happened recently) then the proceeds should be used entirely to make reparation to the victims of crime.

This revocation of rights should not be permanent, but prisoners would have to earn the right to have them back, by achieving and sustaining pre-defined standards of behaviour. This has the benefit of providing both the carrot and the stick, for any recidivism should then result in any rights won being revoked.

The major problem here is that by the time offenders get involved in the penal system, they already have little or no real sense of self-worth or else a distorted sense of self-worth determined by a perverted value system based on their membership of a gang or the extent to which they make their stand against authority.

The only way to solve this has to be to find a way that starts to reinforce the positive. Let's look at some of the issues described earlier in this book and see how we could do this.

EDUCATION

Dealing with children and young people as it does, education is one field where you would certainly expect these principles to apply. Yet, despite the best efforts of some very dedicated people, it is a field where the results are very variable and overall standards appear to be falling. There is more and more for children to learn, but the overwhelming impression is that the product emerging from our schools is less well-equipped than before. I find it appalling that students embarking on a university career are now expected to do a "foundation year" - a year that actually does not count towards their degree, but which is intended to sift out those who can go forward from those who cannot. I have two issues with this.

1. It inevitably has to debase the quality of the final degree, since students surely cannot now cover the same ground in two years that they would previously have covered in three.

2. The universities are now being expected to undertake a function that was previously the responsibility of the school system. This is more costly for society as a whole as:

   - Children learn more easily when they are younger.

   - University is more expensive than school.

   - Students who do not have the aptitude for university are incurring significant debt to find this out.

I suspect that one reason for this is declining standards of discipline. This is partly because, instead of reinforcing classroom discipline in the way our parents would have, modern parents often take the child's side and so undermine the teacher's authority. There appears to be little collective discipline, with less of a deterrent to bad behaviour or performance. Some may argue that the positive incentive to do well has also been removed by the example of parents living on welfare and the difficulty of getting work and/or the need for, and cost of, further education. On the other hand others might argue that pupils today get encouraged too much for mediocre or poor work which ultimately simply results in lower standards.

Whatever your perspective on this, the facts described in Chapter 8 speak for themselves and standards do appear to be declining – as any honest teacher will admit. One has to feel sorry for students who do perform well, only to be barraged with reports about how much easier exams have become and how standards are falling. This detracts from any sense of achievement they should feel.

To the extent they aren't already in place or are not consistently applied some ideas that might help turn this situation around would be:

- Positively reinforcing learning as a meaningful and enjoyable activity in its own right and not just a means to an end. This requires greater flexibility in approach with recognition of the fact that pupils have different capabilities and learn at a different rate.

- Involving the students who learn more quickly in the teaching of those who are finding things more difficult. They say the best way to learn is to explain things and, as long as any sense of superiority is removed, this will help cement the knowledge for the former while helping break the mental barriers for the latter.

- Finding ways to involve parents more in their children's learning in a way that allows them to help, without them feeling inadequate or that they are being shown up in their children's eyes. Parents need to recognise that a shared experience can make the parent-child bond even stronger. (If the child is helping teach the parent – or believes they are – it might even provide the stimulation and positive reinforcement needed to encourage greater participation.)

- Standards that are more clearly defined and set at a higher level, but without the same rigid time constraints.

- Removing the stigma of failure. This is a massive demotivator and non-achievement can be handled more sensitively in a way that recognises individuality without demeaning the student.

- Annual contracts signed between schools and parents setting out:
  - Expectations, both in terms of academic achievements and social behaviour; and
  - Explanations of what is required to meet these expectations; and
  - Consequences if these expectations are not met, including the courses of action that will be taken.

- De-compartmentalising education. It is ridiculous, in an age where the importance of lifelong learning is becoming increasingly important, that education is administered by several different government ministries. More needs to be done to integrate learning into one seamless, modular system so that achievements – academic and practical – can be recognised and built on.

Coincidentally, I met someone recently whose work bears out my theory that a strong, positive sense of self-worth needs in part to be shaped by our education system in order to contribute to improving our individual responses to many of our social challenges. David Lett has spent many years researching the meaning behind behaviour and causes of behaviour and has recently launched something he calls "Proactive Living Skills (PALS)". This entails working with young people at three levels:

1. Physical - dealing with experiences, influences, life events and encounters.

2. Psychological - dealing with attitudes, behaviours, habits and choices made.

3. Philosophical - dealing with values, emotions and motivators.

Early results with this programme in secondary schools have apparently shown a remarkable impact and are very encouraging for the future. Interestingly, the PALS approach has simultaneously boosted many teachers' confidence, indicating that our current systems of teacher development could be strengthened by helping teachers shape a stronger sense of self-confidence when teaching or when facilitating lessons on life-skills, social or emotional development.

It would seem that the focus for schools and teachers is actually made harder by the government focus on measurements and pass rates and parents who push much of the learning and development onto the schools and abrogate their own responsibilities. Parents are still the primary role models for children and we need to understand that it is ultimately one of the most fundamental roles we have in life. None of us is born with a manual on raising children and yet we seem to expect to "pick it up" as we go along, and parent training classes are seen more as an admission of failure than an essential part of our own development. If we want our schools to do a better job we have to do more ourselves to facilitate this.

PARENTING

Babies, like puppies, aren't just for Christmas and, also like puppies, need to be cleaned up after, metaphorically speaking. In other words, parents need to accept that they are responsible for the way their children behave in public. Too often today parents seem able to metaphorically shrug their shoulders and say, "What can I do?" This is exacerbated once children turn 16 and too many parents appear to simply wash their hands of their children immediately they legally become adults.

Every parent has the right to bring up their children in their own way. This also has to take account of children's need to develop into independent adults with their own characters and personalities. These rights need to be protected, but not necessarily enshrined to the extent they sometimes are and legal maturity needs to be recognised as an arbitrary 'line in the sand' that is not necessarily appropriate in every instance.

Parents are recognised as legally responsible for their children until they become adults in their own right. However, this legal responsibility needs to be broadened to include a moral responsibility for their children's behaviour. Children with anti-social behaviour who are sentenced to ASBOs do not suddenly become delinquent. There are signs pointing to it all along, and earlier action can prevent this becoming the social problem it has. I cannot help wonder if this is not partly due to too much centralisation of government. Be that as it may, communities need to rediscover their moral courage and take steps to reverse this trend.

To the extent they aren't already in place or are not enforced rigorously enough, the following steps might help in this regard:

- Greater interaction between schools and parents as outlined under education above. Schools should be entitled to demand and expect greater co-operation from parents. After all they are performing a service for those pupils on behalf of the parents.

- Where interaction with parents does not result in improved behaviour, serious misdemeanours and constant behavioural problems should be escalated to social services or the local police, as appropriate.

- Members of the community should have a 'whistle-blowing' line where they can report incidents of unruly, loutish, anti-social or criminal behaviour. Even if they cannot be named every effort should be made to establish the offender's identity. In such cases the school authorities, social services or police, as appropriate, should take the appropriate follow-up action.

- Parents should be legally required to pay for the costs of any damage and/or the administrative costs of calling in the community authorities. If they cannot afford to do so, they should then be required to contribute in others ways to compensate, in some form of community service.

- Parents should be held jointly responsible for any community costs incurred by their children for up to (say) 7 years after their child achieves their legal majority.

These steps are almost entirely reactive, and while they will all help deter bad behaviour, they all deal with past bad behaviour. More methods of encouraging positive behaviour also need to be found. As always it is more difficult to think these up, and it will require more creative thinking than I can offer. PALS type programmes will certainly help, but it also requires more community and inter-community competitions for standards of behaviour, with prizes being awarded for such things as (say):

- The school with the least number of truancies;

- The school with the most improved behaviours;

- The community with the lowest level of police or social callouts; etc.

The list is virtually endless, but it should be something that the community decides for itself and to which it commits itself - after first assessing the potential negative consequences that could arise. This will also help improve the sense of community and increase the level of grass root involvement in the community.

The overriding goal here should be to make motherhood and fatherhood more valued institutions and provide parents with more tools to play their vital part in raising their children, carefully balancing their rights with their obligations.

Raising children today has become more challenging without the extended family network and older generation support there once was. We need to find new answers to compensate for this. Again I am not really qualified to put forward any specific suggestions, but one possible solution might be to find a way in which families could "adopt grandparents" and thus make older people with no family nearby feel more useful. With their own experience of raising children they could:

- Help take up the "after school care" slack that so many working mothers face.

- Provide more tender, thoughtful care in the child's own environment than any sort of after school club.

- Reduce the social problems of "latch-key" children.

- Instil a greater respect for older people in young children.

- Improve their own quality of life and health by being made to feel more useful.

- Reduce the community costs for senior citizens.

Ultimately it comes back to the fact that being a parent is one of the most important - and most fulfilling - roles we have in life, and we need to do more to both encourage parents to recognise this and ensure that they are equipped and able to develop the confidence and self-worth to undertake the role properly and to ensure that children reap the benefits of good parenting. Good behaviour and a sense of their own worth are far more important barometers of a child's development than mere good grades. There can be no 'cookie-cutter' approach to raising children, but it might be a start to encourage all parents to undergo parenting classes when bad (severely anti-social) behaviour surfaces amongst their children.

WELFARE & SOCIAL BENEFITS

Long-term benefits should be anathema to any self-respecting society or any individual, except in cases of certified mental or physical disability. Accordingly they should be eliminated as a matter of priority. This will require:

- Recognising and redefining benefits as a valid means to help people who have encountered hard times. These may be as a result of any one of a defined list of unfortunate circumstances, preferably but not necessarily, not of their own making.

- Changing the legislation to set an upper limit on the time for which benefits will be paid.

- Mental or physical disability to be independently certified by a medical board with no knowledge of, or personal connection, to the individual. Unfortunately this is necessary because too many doctors do this for their patients when there is no real cause to do so. This is particularly true of doctors providing "sick notes" to get people out of work for stress or back pain issues, where the medical profession seems to rely totally on the patient's word. In situations where a person is already working and gets a medical certificate for a lengthy lay-off on medical grounds the employer, or their health insurance company, should be legally entitled to insist upon the same conditions.

- Providing more generous benefits during the time they are claimed. This will allow the claimant the opportunity to take the necessary action to lift themselves out of the situation, without suffering any erosion of their personal worth. For example to undertake a registered full-time training course in order to secure employment by the time the period elapses.

- Limiting the number of times any one person can claim benefits, and/or (unless there are exceptional circumstances such as an employer going out of business) specifying a minimum period of not less than 5 years before they can claim again. In the event of more than one claim the benefit should be restricted to only a fixed proportion of the original benefit.

- In the event that a claimant is still unable to find regular employment at the end of any claim period they will be required to accept a role in the community at the prevailing rate while they continue to look for suitable work. If they refuse to do so and/or fail to perform those duties properly, they shall forfeit all right to any further help.

Benefits for single mothers is a subject that needs special consideration. PALS based education should go a long way towards giving young girls greater self-respect and make them less susceptible to getting into such situations, but it won't be enough on its own. I do not know enough about the existing programmes to make any detailed recommendations here, but I would suggest that, as a fundamental first step, legislation be passed immediately to take away the "right" of young single mothers having babies to automatically be given free housing. This is unquestionably a 'consequence' that reinforces the wrong sort of behaviour.

The original aim to reduce poverty is noble, but I suspect that the longer term result is actually the direct opposite.

HEALTH

The cost of 'health provision' is one of the single biggest costs faced by any society. There are two fundamental reasons for this:

1. The medical field has become one of the deities of modern civilisation and the costs of health care provision have become exorbitant.

2. We have tried to take away the financial risks associated with ill-health, so that the unfortunate are not disadvantaged compared to the fortunate.

Forget the irony of the fact that, as the generation with the highest living standards and the most advanced technology in history, we also suffer more ill-health than any generation in history; the simple fact is that we cannot afford it. If the individual struggles to afford his healthcare, then it seems to me inevitable that it is only a matter of time before society as a whole is unable to do so.

It is no coincidence that our health is not as a good as our forebears'. The word health is rooted in the word "wholeness" and the self-absorption and lack of thought for others previously described, also effectively means we are not complete as people. Thus it seems inevitable that we have health problems. Yet health is intensely personal, and we are all ultimately responsible for our own healthcare. So why should we look to government for this? It is again consistent with a tendency to shoulder blame and leave things to others that we should even have the term 'healthcare provision' and be looking to government to cover these costs on our behalf.

Obesity, stress, alcohol and smoking related diseases make up the bulk of our healthcare spending, and yet all these problems are intrinsically self-inflicted. So why should society at large pick up the bill for this? Yet, regardless of the rights or wrongs of this, the fact remains that they are all costly and we need to take steps to bring these costs down.

One particular area where affirmative action can be taken is sexually transmitted diseases (STDs). Reports indicate that cases of these are increasing significantly. This is mind-boggling in a world of mass communication where sex education is so strongly championed and widely taught. Once again this seems to point to an uncaring society where people are looking for instant gratification and thinking only of themselves. In order to deter unsafe sexual practices and disease being spread urgent action is necessary. Any solution here needs to balance the need for early action with reinforcement of education that actions have consequences and people have to be accountable for their actions.

Generally, however, we once again need to think and act outside the box. Higher excise duties on alcohol and tobacco have hardly had any deterring effect while putting health warnings on cigarette packets has not significantly reduced the number of people who smoke. Threatening to charge people more if they fall ill is similarly unlikely to succeed, for probably the same reasons. Once again the root causes of many of these problems boil down to a poor self-esteem and so the ultimate solution has to revolve about helping people feel better about themselves. This will again be more easily done if approached from a community perspective and by stimulating people to be more involved in and/or to contribute more to the community. Fundamentally there is little difference between changing anti-social behaviour and changing an addiction or over-indulgence. Thus many of the points made above will apply here too. There may be some overlap when anti-social behaviour can have health consequences and in such instances it may be possible to use stronger deterrents.

POLICING

One area where this may be possible is policing. For example the line is very blurred as to whether binge drinking and being drunk and disorderly is anti-social behaviour, a health risk or simply a 'criminal' act. At the end of the day, however, the definition does not really matter, but the offender needs to learn that the action has consequences. Thus the consequences of someone binge drinking and being apprehended need to be brought home and the person learn that this behaviour is unacceptable. This could be brought home quite simply in the local community by any one or more of:

- Charging the offender for the costs of the police time.

- Making the offender pay for any damage that they cause.

- Making the offender spend time cleaning up after themselves and/or others who behave this way.

There are no clear boundary lines in any of the issues described above, or indeed in this book as a whole. Everything is integrated and somehow connected to everything else. Thus the points and the suggestions should be considered inter-changeable and readily applied to other situations if it is thought they will have the desired affect.

LIBERTY, FRATERNITY, EQUALITY

We began with a look at democracy and some of its shortcomings and it may be as well to come full circle and end there too. The above trinity has come to represent the battle cry of the French Revolution and encapsulate all that democracy is about. But it is important to understand their implications.

Liberty means the freedom to be ourselves, to say what we think and act the way that we want, without any expectation of being constrained simply because someone else doesn't think or feel the same.

Fraternity means that notwithstanding the rights our freedoms bestow, we do not have the right to disregard others. Our actions ultimately still have to conform to what is the greatest good, and we are expected to look after the interests of our fellow human being just as we would our own – a bit like that second great commandment I wrote about earlier.

Equality means that we all have the same rights and that no one person's rights exceed or supersede those of any other.

We need to go back to these and make sure that they underpin our modern democracy, both our self-government and our national government. After all if we cannot govern ourselves properly we can hardly complain when we have a poor government. Somehow these primary values seem to be forgotten today. The claim that we are too self-absorbed suggests that fraternity has definitely been forgotten.

In fact the balance between liberty and fraternity probably creates the single biggest challenge to democracy. Certainly in our age, the balance between personal rights and 'community' rights is one of the thorniest issues. Technology is ubiquitous but it also makes it increasingly difficult to secure our personal information. It creates the possibility of crime on an absolutely unprecedented scale. At the same time, security issues and the cost of policing 'demand' that greater use is made of it.

Consequently we have already seen some erosion of our personal rights as anti-money-laundering practices become more rigidly enforced. This, however, remains the thin edge of the wedge and just this last week-end there were reports that under European Union rules police are entitled to "hack into" personal emails at will without any requirement for any sort of warrant. This certainly makes a mockery of any privacy and data protection laws and is likely to once again increase opposition to the EU and what can be argued as its fundamentally anti-democratic practices.

A particularly thorny issue here in Britain at present is a government proposal to introduce compulsory ID cards. Civil Rights groups are violently opposed to this and see it as a further infringement on personal rights, but clearly security issues indicate that there is some justification for something of this nature. It will be interesting to see how this one pans out, particularly in light of government's recent track record which suggests that it is totally incapable of properly managing personal data and its security.

Civil Rights groups also protest against such issues as personal DNA samples being kept too long in police files after it has been established that there is no case to answer. This highlights the extent to which the principles of personal rights are championed and to which they perhaps need to be. It clearly points to an almighty tussle looming. Personally, however, I anticipate that security needs and the increasing costs of policing will win the day. To this end, I would suggest that the system of registering births and deaths will likely be expanded to included DNA samples being taken at both times, as well as when people migrate. This will result in a national database of this information, which will make police forensic work much easier and help ensure that criminals are identified more easily and at less cost.

The story with equality is similar. Certainly in pushing our own thoughts and opinions, we sometimes seem to completely forget that our brother man's opinion carries an equal weight to our own. However, here it perhaps runs deeper than being forgotten, but it is also misunderstood. Maybe the political emphasis on equality has shifted too far towards the expectation that all people should be equal. The fact is that we are not all equal and never will be. Our very individuality insures that. Different talents and different capabilities mean that in any particular situation no two people will ever be the same, and therefore by definition they will not be equal. Rather it makes more sense that the principle behind equality is in fact that people shall all have equal opportunity. Even this might be the impossible dream, not only because circumstance might always dictate otherwise, but because individual people will achieve different outcomes from the same opportunity.

This is an important point to distinguish. Consequently, any democratic society should not be striving that "all men should be equal" but rather that "all men should have equal opportunity".

This is certainly an impossible goal, but it is one that any free-thinking person who is committed to the cause of democracy would be happy to accept, regardless of whether they are 'left' leaning socialists or 'right' leaning capitalists. It is therefore the ideal starting point for any attempt to reshape the future.

We have seen that both socialism and capitalism have failed badly. Consequently the time is ripe to find a new way forward. The problem is that each philosophy has raised its own expectations amongst its supporters and failure has left each disillusioned. Failure has a nasty after-taste and for each one of us, it erodes our self-belief and hence our sense of our self-worth. Right now the world as we know it is plagued by systems that are perpetuating this self-doubt. Historical systems and methods have been built one on the top of the other in much the same way that city after city was built upon ancient Troy. The problem is that the weaknesses have continued to be built upon and as they do, they remain buried. So the consequences continue to mount.

It is these consequences that are now starting to make life very uncomfortable for humankind. They are heating the water, and unless we wake up to that fact and do something, we could end up like the frog in the analogy threading this book. But humans are not frogs. We have the intelligence, compassion and strength of purpose to ensure this. But in order to do so we need to recognise that "there is a spirit" in man and do all we can to kindle the feeling of worth that will ensure it.

CHAPTER TWELVE

The Credit Crunch

"Only a crisis – real or perceived – produces real change. When that crisis occurs the action taken depends on the ideas that are lying around."

MILTON FRIEDMAN

I don't think there is much doubt that the global economy is experiencing a crisis right now and that 'real change' is required. Unfortunately there do not seem to be many new ideas 'lying around'. Certainly I would be less likely to be writing this book if I felt there were.

What I find particularly troubling, however, are the reports that attempt to pass the current economic crisis off as just another recession, and that suggest it is just a matter of time until things improve. There is enough doom and gloom without adding to it, but without being unduly pessimistic, that is precisely the kind 'frog-in-the-water' thinking that needs to be exposed. Good times will return, but only when we face up to reality and address the root causes and change our systems.

I have referred to the government bailouts of the banking fraternity already, but it is time to look at them in a little more depth. I readily confess to being naïve and not understanding economics properly, but I have yet to be convinced that anyone does. In fact as a friend of mine put it, *"We have been struggling to understand economics for a fraction of the time we have been studying the weather and we are no more adept at the long time forecasts for weather than we are for the economy. We feel that like other sciences we should be able to make predictions and the fact is, despite all the PhDs we cannot."* Once again it seems to me that you can get a good general understanding by bringing it down to the personal level. So let's draw a simple analogy for what has happened.

A SIMPLE ANALOGY

Imagine your friend approaches you and asks to borrow £1,000. You know that he is going through hard times and you want to help so you decide to go ahead and lend the money. Only you don't have the £1,000 so you borrow the money from your parents, in order to help your friend out. Your parents happily lend you the money without any questions because they love you and that's what parents do. Then one day, your first friend turns up and says he doesn't have the money to repay you. Of course this leaves you in a bit of a hole! Your parents need to be repaid, but you don't have the money.

Your friend doesn't have it, you don't have it and your parents don't have it. So who has gained? The recipient of the original £1,000 from your friend! Who is hurting? Just your parents, because they were the only ones who ever really had the money to begin with.

Now imagine that your sister needs to borrow £1,000. Your parents no longer have the £1,000 to give her, but because they lent you that amount, they feel they have to be fair and lend it to her. So what do they do? They approach you and tell you that you need to repay the money immediately, even if the only way you can do that is to borrow it yourself from some other source. Because you cannot do it on your own you approach your girlfriend. She in turn has to go to her rich uncle and borrow the money from him, to enable you to give it to your parents to give to your sister.

Who has gained here? Whoever is the recipient of the money paid by your sister. Have your parents gained? Not really, they still have the same risk they did when they first lent you the money, should your sister prove unable to pay. Meanwhile your girlfriend, who was only vaguely aware of the situation when you got into your original predicament, is now paying off the loan for which she received no benefit other than your gratitude. And of course she is dependent on your sister to pay her.

Apply this now to the commercial world. You and your friend still feature, but remain indigent. The banks now substitute for your parents. Having lent out money rather unwisely in the first place, they are now effectively being bailed out by your girlfriend or her rich uncle, who, of course, represent the man-in-the-street and the taxpayer respectively getting on with their own lives and initially unaffected by the banks' maladministration. The rich uncle however, is now providing the money that he might have better invested elsewhere.

The analogy may be vastly over-simplified and exaggerated, but it serves to make the point. In any past recession the banks simply have to swallow their losses and provide the further funding for future loans. Thus it is this huge government bailout that makes this recession so different from anything in the past. The key point here, which is not particularly well illustrated in the analogy, is that there is a significant long-term future cost. The money being paid by the taxpayer is money that is actually required for all the other issues we have been looking at over the course of this book. Furthermore, unlike the rich uncle, the taxpayer doesn't actually have this money, which necessitates government borrowing it. This means that a significant portion of future revenues will be required to pay the borrowing costs. As we all know this means one of two things:

1. Governments will have less to spend on their other programmes; or

2. The taxpayer will have to pay more to cover those borrowings, because the taxpayer is the person who ultimately funds the government anyway.

This has not happened in past recessions and consequently inevitably means the effects of this one will be much longer lasting than in the past - certainly as long as the decision is made to rescue the banks. In the analogy the decision as to whether or not to go down the chosen route would depend on how badly you wanted your sister to have the money. In the real world the question is fundamentally the same. Your sister represents all the people and businesses who need money to get on with their every day lives.

Governments, legitimately, point out that without this injection the economy will grind to a halt and it is vital to get the economy operating 'normally' as quickly as possible. There are, however, two questions that are not being asked.

Was the 'normal' model appropriate? Certainly the economy has relied too much on debt to stimulate growth. In which case it is once again clear that we have been kidding ourselves with our false profits.

IS THERE NOT A BETTER WAY?

I don't wish to harp any more on the issue of false profits, but the second question is a pretty vital one that deserves more consideration; especially in light of the already high levels of debt at which most western countries are operating.

An Escalating Situation

Despite an initial massive bailout, the situation seems to be continuing to deteriorate. Reports indicate that the banks are suddenly once more at risk as further 'toxic loans' continue to come to the surface, and so there are suggestions that another huge bailout is required.

Government ministers are furious at this and seem to think that it is the fault of the banks for having tried to conceal the problem. However, while there is no way the banks can be exonerated of extremely poor, even criminally negligent management, there seems to be no comprehension of the fact that the number of bad debts will rocket as more and more people lose their jobs.

It is all well and good saying there needs to be credit as usual so businesses can operate properly, but if nobody is working there will be no-one to buy their products. And it does not make any sense to say the banks need to be lending more when the population is already crippled by debt.

So what other options are there?

ALTERNATIVE SOLUTIONS

Governments and national banks do not appear to understand the causes of the crisis. The actions they are taking or proposing are very much old school thinking and the standard response to an economic downturn. There seems to be little or no realisation that they are simply extending and compounding the long-term problems by encouraging borrowing at the undesirable levels prior to the collapse of the markets. The scale of the issues has frozen thinking, while the desire to prevent panic has meant it is better to be seen to be doing something, even if it is diametrically opposed to what is really needed, than to vacillate.

The solutions required need to work in the opposite direction to those being proposed.

TIGHTER CREDIT CONTROL

Clearly, there is an urgent need to change the model and the drivers of the capitalist economy. Certainly it is driven by the ability to borrow, but there need to be very clearly defined and enforced limits as to the extent to which people and businesses can borrow. I would recommend that just as no person was allowed to undertake a mortgage with a repayment of more than 30% of their income, so no business should be allowed to leverage more than 30%. If these limits had been enforced many of the mergers and acquisitions we discussed earlier would never have happened. This would likely have significantly reduced the impact in terms of the number of people who are being made redundant as the credit crunch bites.

A DIFFERENT APPROACH

1. To the Banks

Governments appear reluctant to nationalise the banks, despite much debate. This reluctance seems to be misplaced when they are already effectively owned by the taxpayer. So governments should bite the bullet and simply announce the temporary nationalisation of *all* banks. They should place a moratorium on all bank share-dealings, leaving shareholders with their holdings but with no shareholder rights for a period of (say) 3-5 years.

Governments will then be able to appoint their own managers, or to legislate new banking regulations, for the pre-determined period or until such time as:

- New legislation has been passed creating more stringent regulation, including the credit control measures recommended above; and

- They meet the capitalisation criteria for their newly defined, more restricted services.

At this juncture control will be handed back to the shareholders who can once again play their designated role, but without the speculative ambitions of the recent past.

Government will then be able to direct the vital short-term lending needed to ensure that the 'wheels of commerce' do not grind to the feared halt.

2. To the Taxpayer

At present the priority appears to be more on the banks than the individuals. This is understandable but misguided. One suggestion has been that the government might do better to pay the money directly to small businesses or even directly to individual taxpayers rather than the banks. This is the only alternative idea I have encountered but it still requires a cash injection which ultimately does little to change the points made in the analogy above.

I am positive that the same affect could be achieved by simply writing down all existing debt. This will effectively:

- Nullify much of the effect of over-inflated property prices of the past few years, to the extent this has not already happened. It might also create a precedent to make it is less likely to happen again in the future.

- Reduce overall debt repayment and be equivalent to the cash injection that would be required for the banks.

- Have the desired stimulatory results with nothing like the same long-term costs.

This might not do a great deal for the banks and their capitalisation problems, but hey, they are bankrupt anyway! However, the lower balances outstanding might actually help them recover money on loans that they have already had to write-off as irrecoverable.

Actually, this raises a very interesting question as to how much the banks shoot themselves in the foot with their repossession policies? Perhaps, when there is a danger of having one's home repossessed, people are tempted to consider it a lost cause and thus focus more on their immediate survival needs. Consequently, rather than throw more 'good money after bad' they may squirrel away whatever money they do have to enable them to rehabilitate themselves more quickly afterwards. Basically this is not so very different to business executives, when things start to deteriorate, trying to ensure that all the problems they have previously been trying to conceal, are suddenly brought into the open. That way, they can 'take the big hit' as a once off and still look good when they turn the business around, which is always easier from a low starting point.

Maybe passing legislation prohibiting any lender from repossessing any home (or any middle-class or working-class home) when a person gets into debt would:

- Encourage more prudent lending policies to begin with.

- Ensure banks work more closely with their clientele to manage their debts and keep them at an affordable level.

- Prevent the 'bargain hunting' that occurs when people set out to take advantage of other people's misfortunes and minimise any possibility of corruption in the industry that does sometimes occur.

For a bank to write off the difference between a loan balance and the amount received in a fire-sale of the property is not much different to reducing the loan balance or otherwise renegotiating the repayment terms - particularly if a prudent lending policy was used in the first place. The attraction of the former can be in the timing difference for, if the sale is in a subsequent period, it makes the turnaround look more impressive.

3. Prohibit Redundancies

Governments should reinforce these measures by temporarily prohibiting all redundancies. No business will be eligible for a write down of any commercial loan without first undertaking not to lay off any of its workers. Any business that makes people redundant after receiving a loan write-down without a licence to do so, or that claimed a write-down under false pretences, will be prosecuted and required to repay the write-down with a further substantial penalty.

4. Encourage Savings

The present record low interest rates are also counter-productive. They have done nothing to improve the flow of credit, but have killed off any remaining incentive for people to save in the way previous generations did. Investment can only happen when there is saving and 0.3% for balances in excess of £100,000 is ludicrous in the extreme. Particularly when the real need is to reduce 'retail therapy' and encourage saving. The interest rates should be returned to a minimum of 2.5% immediately and legislation passed to prevent it from ever again being made lower than that.

5. Managing All This

The reduction in loan balances will need to be done quickly and require good management. To ensure this and optimise the intended benefit governments will need to take any or all of the following steps:

- Ensure that loan write-downs were limited to one per taxpayer or household, most likely through proper monitoring of social insurance or corporation numbers.

- Ensure that loan write-downs did not exceed the preset limit.

- Set up a temporary task-force (ideally using bankers or other suitably skilled people who have previously been made redundant) to oversee it.

- Prohibit any home repossessions for the duration of the exercise.

- Pass temporary legislation that no business line of credit or overdraft facility may be cancelled or varied for a defined period, in order to give people and businesses a chance to regroup properly.

This is why all the banks should be nationalised until a new banking system is in place.

BENEFITS

The above suggestions are intended to be a basis for discussion rather than a definite solution. Certainly they will not be easy to implement and they may not be practical at all, but at least they give a platform for considering what might be possible. They would certainly offer a number of enormous benefits. The big ones would be:

- There is no additional debt incurred, so the economy will unquestionably be better off in the long term.

- They lay the foundation for some of the other changes suggested to be introduced, particularly the wider introduction of the recognition of people as assets.

- The job losses will be constrained, which will also mitigate the effect of the recession and help turn things around sooner.

- There will be a new model that can be applied in the event of future recessions.

Perhaps, most important of all, it would demonstrate that Governments do not take their taxpayers for granted and really do have the best economic interests in mind. It would help politicians and citizens reconnect and give both sides a stronger feeling of worth.

Finale

A Final Word

"Far and away the best prize that life offers is the chance to work hard at something worth doing."

THOMAS JEFFERSON

Well there is certainly no doubt that there is a grand prize on offer right now. The world is unquestionably in a period of transition. The old economic model is clearly not working and we need to build a new one. We simply have to grasp Einstein's dictum that you cannot fix a problem with the same mentality that caused it, and stop the insanity of trying to do so.

Whether one subscribes to the theory of global warming or not, climate change is undoubtedly demanding that we take greater care of our environment and the earth's fragile ecology. Now, if that is not challenge enough, we are experiencing an economic climate that looks like it may turn out to be the worst since the Great Depression. And, as journalist, author and Peter-Pan-petrol-head Jeremy Clarkson has pointed out, the demise of Concorde was probably the first time in history since the pharaohs that humankind has taken a step backwards technologically. Yet this may all be good news.

Daunting though it certainly is, it is alerting us to the fact that the water has been getting hotter without us being aware of it, and it is giving us the opportunity to act to rectify things. Gradually and painfully we are learning that the 20th Century was perhaps not the grand success we have boasted about. Its excesses are becoming more evident and the great ideologies that defined the last century are being shown to be emperors without clothes. And the conflicts waged in their names appear to be no more justified and to have no more long-lasting merit than any other conflict in history. Can there be any greater tragedy than a good cause that turns out not to be such a good cause? Most lives lost in war prove ultimately to have been lost in vain and yet we persist in finding ever more lethal ways to inflict damage, and at greater cost with greater potential damage to our whole world. How long can this go on?

Just think of the Israeli bombardment of Gaza. Ignoring (conveniently) the political and humanitarian issues involved, the destruction of homes and infrastructure comes at an enormous price. Now that there is a cease-fire the cost of restoration has become a hot political issue, but nothing was ever said while it was going on. Even now there seems to be scant recognition that valuable resources that could be used elsewhere in the world will have to be used to rectify this mess. How long can the world sustain this kind of waste as the earth's resources are used up? How will future generations judge us - not just for this conflict but all the other wanton destruction for national or ideological causes?

In "The Wealth of Nations" Adam Smith identified, Land, Labour and Capital as the three key factors of production. Well, we have mismanaged land to the point that the earth's capability to sustain life as we know it is under serious threat. We have mismanaged capital to the point that we have just witnessed "the greatest episode of value destruction the world has ever known outside of two world wars."[29] That leaves us only with labour.

If we are to wriggle our way out of the mess we have made of things, we are going to have to do more with and for people. We should be better placed to do this than any generation in history. After all it was our generation that called to "ban the

---

[29] Simon Caulkin: "Corporate Apocalypse" article in January 2009 issue of Management Today.

bomb" and introduced "free-love" with the slogan "make love not war" and all the people-based philosophies overseen by a function called "Human Resources". But, wait a minute! This is the same generation that has overseen this massive mismanagement. Maybe the pot did more damage than was thought! Clearly we cannot trust us to take charge now and clean up the mess of our own making. Hopefully we haven't made too much of a mess of raising the next generation to entrust them with making a better fist of things.

However, the tragedy is that we haven't left them much of a framework to build on. As we have seen, the political and ideological frameworks that underpinned socio-economic development have failed dismally, and there are no ideas for new models.

Yet around the world governments are throwing good money at trying to prop up failed companies and a failed monetary system. They seem to have no idea that, now we have removed the dirt from what we thought was an old master, we have discovered a forgery. The brutal fact is that we have continued to build on shaky foundations for hundreds of years, re-plastering and repainting whenever cracks appeared but without ever going back to first principles to ascertain whether what we were doing was justified or whether there was any need to rebuild. I have already questioned the affordability of this, but I also question the thinking behind it. As we have seen, economics is more chaotic than we would like to believe and it seems even the people ostensibly running our economies are at a complete loss and doing whatever has been done in the past because:

- That's what they know; and

- They have to be seen to be doing something.

Conventional wisdom says that governments are the only ones who can lead us out of an economic recession. We have, however, seen that conventional wisdom is more convention and less wisdom. So at the very least government needs to be more open about what it is doing, why and what the ultimate price is going to be. The latest talk is about a "Bad Bank" to take over all the (still yet unidentified) "toxic loans". What on earth will that do, but leave the taxpayer (you and me) with a massive debt and the other banks to carry on as before! (Besides, who would want to work for a "bad bank"?)

Certainly we need to reduce the cost of government and its share of the economy, yet we are actually giving them more power. Methinks this is a dog that won't hunt, yet there appear to be very few alternative suggestions. So, whether you agree with my ideas or not, I hope you will give me the credit for trying.

At the very least I would challenge governments to use the Alistair Lobo "Be Do Have" model introduced in the preface to identify and monitor their purpose, vision, mission and expected outcomes. This would result in a primary role of governments being to protect the environment for which it is responsible and to oversee and monitor the effective use of economic resources. It would also make governments more accountable and provide citizens with a proper means of assessing their performance. Maybe it would even allow us to dispense with party politics completely and all the problems this has created.

At the same time it is manifestly clear that businesses cannot be left to operate the apparently untrammelled way in which it has. There is no doubt that many businesses, typified as we have seen by the financial institutions and the motor industry, have become so obsessed with profits and creating shareholder value that they have forgotten their raison d'être; their very essence. What is this but their purpose? I therefore think that as a minimum requirement, every single business should be required to submit an annual "Be Do Have" return with its annual return. This should make clear that the leaders running the business know what they are doing and why, and any misstatement or deviation from that should be a criminal offence. With questions needing to be asked as to how the accounting profession allowed the situation to deteriorate to the extent it has, one could legitimately challenge why, but there should also be a requirement for this statement to be independently verified.

Of course you can argue that companies already do this, and their mission statement covers this ground. However, they are not the same thing. As you may recall from Alistair's model, the mission comes after the purpose and the vision. A mission statement, even if it is not subverted to be little more than a propaganda exercise or a slogan, is at a lower level. It addresses the what and the how issues, but doesn't touch on the why. And, as we have seen, when we forget the why the whole value change and modus operandi gets totally screwed up.

At the same time, the concept of shareholder value needs to be re-evaluated and its commercial dominance needs to be severely trimmed. There is no obvious alternative to profit as a measure of corporate performance and shareholders do need to have a proper reward for their risk. However, greater focus needs to be given to the economic use of resources and businesses need to be more accountable for this. The triple bottom-line thus needs to be given greater prominence and legal standing. It should never be forgotten that a business exists to provide a service and has an obligation to do that effectively, efficiently, and ethically.

Mergers and acquisitions need to be subjected to far greater regulatory review and their numbers drastically reduced. Merger and acquisition activity in the US grew tenfold from 2% to 21% of the US GDP between 1980 and 2000,[30] and it is

---

[30] Source: Management Today January 2009

manifestly clear that many of these were ultimately not in the best interests of either the shareholders or the employees. The scale of the downturn and the impact of mass failures on the wider economy suggest that it would be better to spread the economic risks a little wider. It is unhealthy for a company to grow too big, and more needs to be done to restrict growth. Indeed, many argue that it is big business "Corporate America" that is really running things in the US and hence in much of the world. That is not a debate I want to get into, but I would suggest that the fact that it can even be claimed is indicative of a problem. It certainly reinforces my case about the failings of democracy.

Management wings also need to be clipped. It is difficult to prove categorically, but hindsight would suggest that much of the merger and acquisition growth was actually stimulated by executive ego as much as anything. Executives have arguably been the least affected of all by the recent financial disasters. Shareholders have lost their investments, and employees have lost their livelihoods, but executives have been better cushioned from the extremes of these consequences by the size of the pay packages in preceding years. Granted a significant proportion of their pay has been in shares and share options - according to Standard & Poor's, stock options granted to US executives in 2002 amounted to 20% of all corporate profits[31] - but this is still only a portion of their cash earnings. Given that between 2003 and 2007 US companies bought back $1.7 *trillion* of their own stock[32] it is fair to assume that many executives were able to liquidate their holdings. This does seem rather ironic when much of the blame can be laid at their door. As Professor Julian Birkinshaw of the London Business School pointed out, *"the*

---

[31] Ibid

[32] Ibid

visible hand of management failed too. Most big companies just failed to do what big companies are supposed to do. "[33] Maybe we need to restate what it is that big companies *are* supposed to do, at the same time remember that it is the executives who control the doing. It seems totally incongruent with everything we believe and value that big companies should have such massive power when their contribution to society as a whole is proportionately small.

Executives should also be required to have personal "Be Do Have" statements which are subjected to independent review. On top of that their total earnings should be legally restricted to either:

- A maximum figure in relation to the organisation's profits; or

- A maximum of the total organisational payroll; and/or

- A maximum multiple of the lowest salary in the company.

This last is not a new concept. Ben and Jerry had a rule when they started their ice-cream business that no-one could earn more than 5 times what the lowest paid person earned. Unfortunately, that rule was apparently 'lost' when they were taken over.

Clearly management's role as the custodian of the business needs to be restored. A good first step would be to make any payment in shares or share options illegal. Any violation of any of these regulations should be a criminal offence and incur a significant penalty, including a mandatory jail sentence and a life ban from any further executive position.

As suggested previously, derivative financial products should also be made illegal together with dealing in them. Similarly,

---

[33] Ibid

any form of option or short selling. It is quite apparent that these distort the market. They have effectively turned banks and stock exchanges into betting shops. Thus such activity - or any attempt to create a similar activity in any form - should be made illegal too. Once again violation of any of the laws should incur heavy penalties.

The whole credit crunch proves that greed and white-collar crime can have far reaching effects and thus regulations should be rigorously enforced. It should be mandatory to investigate *any* suspected breech and proper investigative techniques put in place to allow this.

The ideas I have put forward above are a mixture of proactive and reactive steps, entailing both positive and negative reinforcement to inspire better behaviour and deter bad behaviour. They all, however, need to be brought together and the best way to do that is to come back to Khalil Gibran's words:

"Work is love made visible."

This simple statement is incredibly profound. It encapsulates the concept that work is not the nine-to-five bondage that we have made it, but the way in which we express who we are. It goes way, way beyond the principle that was ingrained into us by our parents that, "If the job is worth doing, it is worth doing properly!" We are all familiar with the concept of "a labour of love" used to depict the craftsmanship and effort that has been put into something. Well, this statement argues the corollary, that our work itself evidences what we put into it. Everything we do expresses something about who we are. So, every task that is done unwillingly, or that is rushed or skimped, not only short-changes those for whom it is done but the person doing it. It detracts from our feeling of worth. On an individual basis this may not matter but, as it multiplies and becomes a habit, it has a demoralising and demotivating effect on everything we do. Everything becomes "a job" and we start to lose our satisfaction and with it our joy.

A story will perhaps explain this better. My friend Alexander Kjerulf, The Chief Happiness Officer, in his campaign to bring more happiness to the workplace, always quotes the small 7-man company in Ohio that offers a dog-walking service. As he 'punnily' puts it, "cleaning up after other people's dogs is a pretty shit job!" Yet the people who do it absolutely love their work and know their work is valuable. Why? Because they are helping improve the quality of life for elderly people who cannot take proper care of their own pets, but for whom the dogs make an enormous difference to their quality of life.

So the purpose is not to clean up dog pooh, but to make people happy. Now isn't that a worthwhile purpose? You can understand why those dog-walkers have a feeling of worth, probably far greater than any of the bankers with their ruined reputations and tawdry, undeserved millions.

Referring back to "Growing Your Own Heroes"[34] the authors quote Colin Potter, the Chief Executive of Uniworld, which was one of their case studies, as saying *"Good service is only ever provided by people who care. People only care if they are given reason to care. Usually that stems from a sense of belonging and understanding. They feel that they belong, because they have a clear autonomous role. They understand because they share in the goals of the company. If the company is successful, they will share in that success both financially and emotionally. They feel valued because they are valued. These people deliver good service because they genuinely feel good about themselves and the company they represent."*

What more need I say? The Towers Perrin global workforce survey that we studied earlier showed that only 10-30% of people globally are engaged in their work. That means 70-

[34] "Growing Your Own Heroes: The Commonsense Way to Improve Business Performance" John J Oliver & Clive Memmott, Oaktree Press © 2006

90% of us do not have the same feeling of worth as those dog-walkers or the workers at Uniworld. Would you not agree that this is a very sad state of affairs? I would even suggest it is a massive problem.

I would very much like to think that some of the suggestions put forward in this book will help solve that problem. They are limited in so far as they still work within the confines of the current model and may not be visionary enough to form the basis of the more ideal economy. Nevertheless they might help to form a bridge for the transition. We certainly need to start doing something, and the sooner the better.

It is all very well blaming greedy bankers for the economic mess we are in, but the fact is we are all equally culpable. We have passively watched what has been going on and done nothing to prevent it. We have even contributed by getting caught up on the treadmill and living beyond our means. It's all very well trying to keep up with the Joneses, but the problem is, when the Joneses go bust, we go bust with them. That is what is happening at present. The fact of the matter is that the government bailouts are simply a stalling tactic, delaying us from actually suffering the consequences of our folly.

The tragedy of it all is that, despite everything, we are no happier for it all. We have sold our souls and jeopardised the livelihoods of future generations for stuff that hasn't even made us happy. We haven't really understood that success cannot be bought.

Everyone has their own definition of success, but it would be hard to beat "The ultimate achievement of a purpose" as an all-purpose, general definition. There are three fundamental aspects to achieving personal success:

1. Identifying your talents and what you like to do to use those talents.

2. Working hard to develop and use those talents.

3.   Appreciation for the way you have used those talents.

If we apply this to those dog-walkers, we can identify that they have a simple talent of being good with animals and people, and they work hard to keep the dogs and their owners happy, even when it means more than just exercising the animals. As a result, they have satisfied customers and feel good about themselves. This is a simple example of the "Be Do Have" model and brings us back full circle to where we started. It isn't exactly rocket science. Of course the theory is easier than the practice, but that's where the 2nd part - the doing - comes in. It is the practice that makes perfect and as we develop our perfection so we increase our satisfaction.

This is what philosophers, great leaders and religious teachers have been teaching for millennia; and yet somehow with all our technology we seem to be further removed from it than ever.

So if we want to change the world we have to start with the people, beginning with ourselves. If we are to turn this around we have to develop a stronger feeling of worth in order to re-establish the habit of giving our best. This applies to both us and the people we work with or have working for us. Clearly, this starts with ensuring there is a proper and clear sense of purpose to everything we undertake; and it would seem that the "Be Do Have" approach would be an ideal way to start this. Every one of us should do the exercise for herself or himself.

However, it runs much deeper than a simple personal exercise. It brings us back to Adam Smith and the land, labour, capital balance. Do you remember the explanation of the spiritual and how the 'spiritual' multiplies while nothing else does? Well, this starts with people. It only develops as people are inspired, and thus we need to do more to inspire people, including ourselves. The dwindling of the other two resources and their apparently finite limits, together with the scale of the challenges we face, necessitates making better use of our people.

Ideas are not limited to those who have a house or a car. Or to those who have a vote. On top of that, ideas develop more, bloom and flourish, when they are shared. Consequently the world population presents an almost infinite resource. If the ideas are to be forthcoming that will help us save the world, we have to find a way to harness and empower these people. This means that we need to stop looking on people simply as consumers or potential consumers. There are millions, if not billions, of people in the world who aspire to have the same standard of living that we in the west do. There is no way that we will ever be able to meet these aspirations if we persist with both:

1. The wasteful use of existing resources.

2. The approach of looking at things from the finite.

Certainly we will stand a better chance if we try to channel the enormous potential of all these people. We have to stop the sort of possessive, protectionist thinking, which four thousand years of human history has shown us does not achieve anything. We need to work together to share and develop new ideas that will help us face the challenges depicted in this book and others that I have left out. We need to strip down our existing models and develop new ones.

This process can only begin when we do that. Let's look at a couple of examples of what this means.

Firstly let's look at our waste and its disposal. We are all learning to recycle our rubbish. This is unquestionably a good thing, and something we should have been more aware of a long time ago. Yet how did we become aware of this? Through the water starting to become uncomfortably hot and a few concerned citizens taking up the rallying cry, and politicians turning to it as a way to increase their chances of election.

Yet, it is these same politicians who pass health and safety laws demanding more packaging for our foods, generally very environmentally unfriendly packaging too. Wouldn't it make more sense to tackle the problem at source and demand less packaging and more environmentally-friendly packaging from the companies that pack the goods and or manufacture the packaging? Why do my bananas and apples have to be wrapped in the first place? We grew up with sweets and candies being sold out of jars or containers and we survived. Why do they now all have to be individually wrapped? We protest against atomic power, because of the potential dangers it poses, and instead use more environmentally unfriendly power sources, rather than focussing on developing alternative power sources.

Similarly most efforts to solve the problems of climate change seem to focus on getting us to reduce our carbon emissions. Again, great! But there isn't even agreement on the causes of this climate change: it is another subject where we are hardly any more knowledgeable than we are on economics. And in any case, the general prognosis seems to be that the change is already irreversible and even if we were to stop all our carbon emissions it might be too late. There is certainly every justification for making every effort to reduce the kinds of things that we suspect cause climate change, but we also need to look at the bigger picture. Ideally we should be looking at what we can do to remedy the problem and simply pay Brazil to maintain the rain forests. Instead, however, the world powers negotiate carbon trading, giving businesses and bankers more opportunities to deal in phantasmagorical products, all while the effects persist!

This can only happen in a world where economic value is the ultimate motive and accords with the global imperative. *"Performance can be maximised when one builds up from worth and great potential of each functioning in harmony with the group."* (Ray Carey Democratic Capitalism: The Way to a World of Peace and Plenty P 431) If, as we saw earlier, Carey is right about the extent to which the "market" has been corrupted and the checks and balances of the invisible forces which govern it have been emasculated, then we need to ensure that regulations are put in place to ensure that these forces can never again be subverted; that the "invisible hand" - recognised and acknowledged as sufficient by some of the greatest economic thinkers in history - is allowed to provide the proper checks and balances to maintain equilibrium and prevent "speculators" from becoming too powerful. We need to ensure that the gridlock between the ultra-capitalists (the modern day equivalent of the feudal robber barons) and the collectivists (the so-called liberals who believe in the redistribution of wealth but without recognising the value of individual freedom) is never again allowed to reach the levels it has in the 20th and early 21st Centuries.

My own experience as a manager has taught me the same lesson as Ray Carey, that *"Full potential is reached through individual development in a harmonious whole, because total performance is the sum of individual performance enhanced by the co-operative environment."* (P 420) I therefore concur totally with Carey"s conclusion that the only way forward is by maximising individual freedom and creating the "circle of trust and co-operation" - the attitude of caring and sharing - that *"generate good feelings and foster social cohesion."* (P 425)

In any event, these are the kind of challenges that only people can solve. But in order to do so we have to create a world in which we can co-operate to develop and deliver these new solutions. This can only happen in a world where the United Nations Declaration of Rights includes a more clearly defined, balancing Declaration of Obligations, and where people of all nations forget ideology and start working together from a basis of common purposes and values.

It was Helen Keller who said, *"Many persons have the wrong idea of what constitutes true happiness. It is not attained through self-gratification but through fidelity to a worthwhile purpose."* Perhaps that could be paraphrased as, *"We will never find happiness until we establish a greater feeling of worth."*

Bibliographical Notes

FOREWORD

Karl Paul Reinhold Niebuhr (1892-1971) an American theologian is best known for his study of the task of relating the Christian faith to the realities of modern politics and diplomacy. Quote used is his "Prayer for Serenity."

"Be Do Have" Model is copyright material used by permission of Alistair Lobo of Certain Progress Consultants *www.certianprogress.com*

Abraham Maslow (1908-1970) "The Father of Modern Management & Employee Motivation" First published his hierarchy of needs in a 1943 paper, "A Theory of Human Motivation" which he expanded in his 1962 book, "Toward a Psychology of Being." To find out more about this concept and its subsequent evolution go to *www.maslow.org*

CHAPTER 1

"The art of life lies in a constant readjustment to our surroundings." Okakura Kakuzo (1862-1913) a Japanese scholar who contributed to the development of arts in Japan.

Charles Darwin (1809-1882) British scientist and author of the 1909 book, "The Origin of Species" which first posited the theory of evolution.

"The Age of Unreason" by Charles Handy, British management guru and author, published by Arrow books 1990, first published in 1989

"Calvin & Hobbes" is a comic strip written and illustrated by Bill Watterson, featuring the antics of a young boy Calvin and his stuffed tiger, Hobbes, which gives wonderful insights into everyday life.

"The Fifth Discipline: The Art & Practice of the Learning Organisation" by Peter Senge, published by Century Business Books 1992. Mr Senge is an American scientist and Director of the Center for Organisational Learning at the MIT/Sloan School of Management.

"Insanity is repeating the same thing over and over again and expecting a different outcome", is variously attributed to Benjamin Franklin and HW Longfellow and possibly others.

CHAPTER 2

"I disapprove of everything you say, but will defend to the death your right to say it!" Attributed to Voltaire (Francois-Marie Arouet) but apparently not found in any of his writings.

"No one pretends that democracy is perfect or all-wise. Indeed it has been said that democracy is the worst form of government except all those other forms that have been tried from time to time." Winston Churchill (1874-1965) Britain's war-time Prime-Minister, who in addition to being a former soldier turned politician was also an artist, writer and historian. Quote from Hansard November 11, 1947.

"Liquid Thinking" by Damien Hughes, published by Deanprint © 2005

"Come on then, we need a political punch-up", Lord Saatchi, The Sunday Times, 7th January 2007

"The British People are now so knowledgeable that they approximate to what economists call, 'the perfect market', i.e. perfect knowledge and perfect ability to use it." Ibid

CHAPTER 3

"Normally speaking, it may be said that the forces of a capitalist society, if left unchecked, tend to make the rich richer and the poor poorer and thus increase the gap between them." Jawaharlal Nehru (1889-1964) Indian first and longest serving Prime Minister (1947-1964). The published source for this quote is 'Credo' 'La propri t c'est le vol.' Property is theft.

"Current experience suggests socialism is not a stage beyond capitalism but a substitute for it – a means by which the nations which did not share in the Industrial Revolution can imitate its technical achievements; a means to achieve rapid accumulation under a different set of rules of the game." Joan Robinson (1903-1983) British Economist and author. She made this widely quoted statement in 1960, but I am unable to identify the original source or context.

CHAPTER 4

"Many people feel empty, a world that seemed so strong just collapsed. Forty years have been wasted on stupid strife for the sake of an unsuccessful experiment. The values gathered together have vanished, the strategies for survival have become ridiculous. And so forty years of our lives have become a story, a bad anecdote. But it may be possible to remember these adventures with a kind of irony." George Konrad (1933) Hungarian novelist. While this statement is widely quoted all over the internet I cannot trace its original source or the timing thereof.

"Current experience suggests socialism is not a stage beyond capitalism but a substitute for it – a means by which the nations which did not share in the Industrial Revolution can imitate its technical achievements; a means to achieve rapid accumulation under a different set of rules of the game." Joan Robinson (1903-1983) British Economist and author. She made this widely quoted statement in 1960, but I am unable to identify the original source or context.

"Give a man a fish and you give him a meal; teach a man to fish and you feed him for life." Generally attributed to Lao Tzu (570-490 BC) Founder of Taoism.

"Idleness and pride tax with a heavier hand kings and governments." Benjamin Franklin (1706-1790) One of the Founding Fathers of America and a leading author, printer, satirist, political theorist, politician, scientist, inventor, statesmand and diplomat.

CHAPTER 5

"Every action has an equal and opposite reaction", Isaac Newton's 3rd Law of Motion

"We have nothing to fear but fear itself" Franklin D Roosevelt (1882-1945) 32nd President of the United States. This statement was made in his inaugural address to the nation in March 1933.

"The Value Motive: The ONLY Alternative to the Profit Motive" Paul Kearns © 2007 John Wiley & Sons"

"This book has a single, very simple message. Manage for maximum value." Ibid Page xix

"At the root of this debate, the total package, are the political and economic systems that we choose to run society." Ibid Page xxi Emphasis in the original.

"A motive that simultaneously enriches society materially and spiritually." Ibid Page xxii

"All organisations should be defined by what outputs they are meant to achieve and judged on what scarce resources they use up in achieving these outputs." Ibid Page 19

CHAPTER 6

"The power of tax is the power to destroy." John Marshall (1755-1835) American statesman and jurist who shaped American constitutional law and made the Supreme Court a centre of power, who after serving as Secretary of State was the US Chief Justice from February 4, 1801, until his death in 1835.

"Taxes are the dues that we pay for the privileges of membership in an organised society", Franklin D Roosevelt.

"The hardest thing in the world to understand is the income tax", Albert Einstein (1879-1955) German-born Physicist and originator of the Theory of Relativity.

"Taxman's errors cost us millions." Manchester Evening News, 6 July, 2007

"It seems to me that there must be an ecological limit to the number of paper pushers the earth can sustain, and human civilisation will collapse when the number of, say tax lawyers, exceeds the world's total population of farmers, weavers, fisherpersons and paediatric nurses", Barbara Ehrenreich: in "Premature Pragmatism," The Worst Years of Our Lives, 1991

"The income tax has made more liars out of Americans than golf. Even when you make a tax form out on the level, you don't know when it's through if you are a crook or a martyr," Will Rogers (1879-1935) American actor and humorist, in "The Illiterate Digest" 1924

"No nation ever taxed itself to prosperity," Rush Limbaugh, American radio host and conservative political commentator

"When confronted with American largesse [charitable giving], the British tend to fall back on three face-savers: they're richer than us; they get more generous tax breaks; and they're social climbing. There is some truth in all of these, but they don't go the whole way to explaining why Americans give about three times more to charity, as a proportion of GDP, than we do." Camilla Cavendish: The Times 22nd June, 2006.

"I am proud of paying taxes. The only thing is I could be just as proud for half the money," Arthur Godfrey (1903-1983) American radio and television broadcaster and entertainer.

CHAPTER 7

"The tax collector must love poor people. He is creating so many of them." William E (Bill) Vaughan (1915) American writer and humourist

"Democratic Capitalism: The Way to a World of Peace and Plenty" Ray Carey © 2004 Author House

"Well, we did pay Matthews to keep having children" Sunday Times, 7 December, 2008

"Council pays out £90,000 a year in rent to a mother of four" Sunday Times 21 December, 2008

"Well, we did pay Matthews to keep having children" Sunday Times, 7 December, 2008

CHAPTER 8

"The problem is not that there are problems. The problem is expecting otherwise and thinking that having a problem is a problem." Theodore Rubin (1923) American writer and psychiatrist.

"Conservatives and market fundamentalists have stolen the good phrase free markets, for they pretend to free the world's capital market, while they, at the same time, contradict economic freedom through the reliance on federal insurance, subsidies and bailouts." Democratic Capitalism: The Way to a World of Peace and Plenty P 467 Ray Carey ©2004 Author House.

CHAPTER 9

"Happiness lies not in the mere possession of money; it lies in the joy of achievement, in the thrill of creative effort. The joy and moral stimulation of work no longer must be forgotten in the mad chase of evanescent profits. These dark days will be worth all they cost us if they teach us that our true destiny is not to be ministered unto but to minister to ourselves and to our fellow men." Franklin D Roosevelt: First Inaugural Speech, March 1933

Towers Perrin 2007 Global Workforce Study The largest study of its kind, involving 90,000 people in 18 countries. For details go to *www.towersperrin.com/tp/showhtml.jsp?url=global/publications/gw s/index.htm&country=global*

"The Future of Management" Gary Hamel © 2007 Harvard Business Press

"Lean Organisations Need FAT People (third edition)" Bay Jordan © 2009 Lean Marketing Press

"The key driver to successful implementation is not the sophistication and technical excellence of your structures, but the spirit and intent behind them." "Growing Your Own Heroes: The Common Sense Way to Improve Business Performance" John J Oliver and Clive Memmott Oaktree Press © 2006

"Caught in the death spiral." Sunday Times News Review 14 December 2008

Facts taken from the article "Corporate Apocalypse" published in Management Today: January 2009

"Maximum value can only be achieved by maximising the value of people." Paul Kearns "The Value Motive: The ONLY Alternative to the Profit Motive" © 2007 John Wiley & Sons.

CHAPTER 10

"Faced with a crisis, the man of character falls back on himself. He imposes his own stamp of action, takes responsibility for it, makes it his own." Charles de Gaulle (1890-1970) French General and politician who served as President of France from 1959 to1969.

"While the miser is merely a capitalist gone mad, the capitalist is a rational miser." Karl Marx, Capital Volume 1 Chapter 4, 1867.

"A business that makes nothing but money is a poor kind of business." Universally attributed to Henry Ford but no original source identified.

"The noblest charity is to preclude a man from accepting charity, and the best alms are to show and enable a man to dispense with alms." Moses Maimonides (1135-1204) Jewish Rabbi and Philosopher

"Prisoners turning down the chance of early release." Headline in The Times, 4 June, 2008.

"Ex-con tries to break back into jail" Headline in Daily Mirror, 18 August, 2006

"It is not only for what we do that we are held responsible, but also for what we do not do." Moliere (Jean-Baptiste Poquelin - 1622-1673) French playwright and actor

CHAPTER 11

"Man must cease attributing his problems to his environment, and learn again to exercise his will and his personal responsibility." Albert Schweitzer (1875-1965) German theologian, musician, philosopher and physician, famous for his medical clinic in Gabon.

Author's Note: Research on this quote shows that it has also been reported slightly differently to my original source as "Man must cease attributing his problems to his environment, and learn again to exercise his will - his personal responsibility in the realm of faith and morals."

David Lett: Proactive Livings Skills (PALS) *www.newmeaning.co.uk*

CHAPTER 12

"Only a crisis - real or perceived - produces real change. When that crisis occurs the action taken depends on the ideas that are lying around." Milton Friedman (1912-2006) American Nobel Prize-winning economist, statistician and public intellectual.

FINAL WORD

"Far and away the best prize that life offers is the chance to work hard at something worth doing." Theodore Roosevelt (1858-1919) 26th President of the United States form a speech made in 1903.

"The greatest episode of value destruction the world has ever known outside of two world wars." Simon Caulkin: "Corporate Apocalypse" article in January 2009 issue of Management Today.

"Merger and acquisition activity in the US grew tenfold from 2% to 21% of the US GDP between 1980 and 2000" Source: Management Today January 2009

"According to Standard & Poor's, stock options granted to US executives in 2002 amounted to 20% of all corporate profits" Ibid

"Between 2003 and 2007 US companies bought back $1.7 *trillion* of their own stock." Ibid

"The visible hand of management failed too. Most big companies just failed to do what big companies are supposed to do." Professor Julian Birkinshaw of the London Business School: Ibid

"Work is love made visible." "The Prophet" Khalil Gibran (1883-1931) Lebanese-American artist, poet and writer.

Alexander Kjerulf, The Chief Happiness Officer, Author of "Happy Hour is 9 to 5!" *www.positivesharing.com*

"Good service is only ever provided by people who care. People only care if they are given reason to care. Usually that stems from a sense of belonging and understanding. They feel that they belong, because they have a clear autonomous role. They understand because they share in the goals of the company. If the company is successful, they will share in that success both financially and emotionally. They feel valued because they are valued. These people deliver good service because they genuinely feel good about themselves and the company they represent." Colin Potter, Chief Executive of Uniworld, quoted in "Growing Your Own Heroes: The Common Sense Way to Improve Business Performance" John J Oliver and Clive Memmott Oaktree Press © 2006

"Performance can be maximised when one builds up from worth and great potential of each functioning in harmony with the group." Democratic Capitalism: The Way to a World of Peace and Plenty P 431 Ray Carey © 2004 Author House

"Full potential is reached through individual development in a harmonious whole, because total performance is the sum of individual performance enhanced by the co-operative environment." Ibid P 420

"Generate good feelings and foster social cohesion." Ibid P 425

"Many persons have the wrong idea of what constitutes true happiness. It is not attained through self-gratification but through fidelity to a worthwhile purpose." Helen Keller, "The Simplest Way to be Happy." 1933

About the Author

Bay Jordan is a baby-boomer, born and raised in what was then Rhodesia (now Zimbabwe) during the last embers of the glory of the British Empire, and in the aftermath of Rhodesia's ill-fated Unilateral Declaration of Independence (UDI). This provided him with a middle-class upbringing in a privileged society with a standard of living that was probably second to none, together with an awareness that it would not last. As it turned out change started happening sooner than expected and he was obliged to combine his accountancy studies with compulsory military duties during the war that followed. The futility of trying to defeat an ideology with a rifle appalled him and he emigrated to South Africa as soon as he had finished his final exams. Slightly more than a decade there further undermined his innate respect for government authority and he emigrated with his family to Canada, before moving to the UK in the mid-nineties. This itinerary and the circumstances of his upbringing, combined with an genetic interest in politics - his great-uncle was deputy-leader of the United Party in South Africa under Sir de Villiers Graaff - has made him very sensitive to socio-political issues, but done nothing to reassure him about the calibre of government. This book is thus a cry for sanity in a world that seems to be unravelling at the seams.

Talk To Bay Jordan

If you would like to know more about the ideas presented in this book, how to take action yourself and how Bay can help you to apply these principles to bring about positive change and improve your organisation's bottom line results by at least 20% then contact him to speak to your organisation at...

www.afeelingofworth.com

Bay provides:

- ✓ Corporate and political change consultancy
- ✓ Human Asset Accounting – raising company value through people
- ✓ Expert writing on social, organisational and economic change
- ✓ Keynote Speeches – based on his revolutionary concepts

LEAN
Organisations
Need

FAT
People

How to Grow Your Human Assets
THIRD EDITION

Bay Jordan

www.bookshaker.com

www.ingramcontent.com/pod-product-compliance
Lightning Source LLC
Chambersburg PA
CBHW070906270326
41927CB00011B/2472